LATINIDAD, IDENTITY FORMATION, AND THE MASS MEDIA LANDSCAPE

Gabriel A. Cruz, PhD

LATINIDAD, IDENTITY FORMATION, AND THE MASS MEDIA LANDSCAPE

Constructing Pocho Villa

The Latinx Studies Collection

Collection Editor

Manuel Callahan

ᴸᴾᴾ

This book is dedicated to Rafael, Raquel, Lucero, Leonardo, Nayeli, and Lucia, whose *nepantlas* share borders with mine.

First published in 2024 by Lived Places Publishing

The author and editor have made every effort to ensure the accuracy of information contained in this publication, but assume no responsibility for any errors, inaccuracies, inconsistencies, and omissions. Likewise, every effort has been made to contact copyright holders. If any copyright material has been reproduced unwittingly and without permission the Publisher will gladly receive information enabling them to rectify any error or omission in subsequent editions.

British Library Cataloguing in Publication Data
A CIP record for this book is available from the British Library

ISBN: 9781915734778 (pbk)
ISBN: 9781915734792 (ePDF)
ISBN: 9781915734785 (ePUB)

The right of Gabriel A. Cruz to be identified as the Author of this work has been asserted by them in accordance with the Copyright, Design and Patents Act 1988.

Cover design by Fiachra McCarthy
Book design by Rachel Trolove of Twin Trail Design
Typeset by Newgen Publishing UK

Lived Places Publishing
Long Island
New York 11789

www.livedplacespublishing.com

Abstract

This volume combines media studies scholarship with autoethnographic storytelling to engage with the construction of *Latinidad* at both the mass-mediated and the individual level. The author synthesizes scholarly literature regarding *Latinidad* as it has been represented through news broadcasts, fictional television, film, superhero narratives, and video games while also incorporating stories from his life that anchor the discussions of each medium in a lived experience. Throughout the volume, a variety of concepts and theories are used to frame each chapter and provide the reader with an academic toolbox, a repertoire of ideas that the reader will be able to apply to the media that they encounter in their day-to-day lives. This approach of utilizing academic media analysis, conceptual frameworks, and personal experience results in critical engagement with the ways in which media informs the personal and collective construction of *Latinidad* while also interrogating the utility of the identity.

Key Words

Latinidad; latinx; media; news; superheroes; fiction; video games; autoethnography; race; whiteness; social constructionism; *nepantla*.

Contents

Learning objectives

After reading this text the reader will be able to:

- Identify how racial and ethnic identities are constructed within the media.
- Critically engage with media artifacts as vehicles of ideologies.
- Interrogate their own sense of *Latinidad*, for those who are members of the Latinx community.
- Reflect on how the media has informed their understanding of Latinx communities, for those who are not Latinx.
- Identify the role of the media as a system for shaping our socially constructed reality.
- Discern between reductive media that further marginalizes racialized groups and media that facilitates humanizing perspectives of those groups.

1
A carpenter's son, an academic toolbox

It might seem counterintuitive, but when you are working on a roof in the warm weather, one of the most important things you can do is wear pants and a long-sleeved shirt as opposed to shorts and a T-shirt. The benefit of doing this is that it protects your skin from the sun. One might think that it would cause you to sweat more, but the truth is that if you find yourself roofing on a summer day in the Southeastern United States, then heavy sweating and dehydration are inevitable. But at 16 years old I had not learned this lesson yet. So, as I worked alongside my dad on the roof of our home adding shingles onto a new office we were building, I struggled in the heat of a North Carolina summer day in 2004. I would later learn about the value of covering up my arms and legs while working with my dad, but not from my dad. Rather, I would learn it from the other Latinos my dad would hire to help build houses, from framing to finishing work. My dad did not wear pants and long sleeves in the warm weather; instead, he opted for a uniform of work boots, jean shorts, a T-shirt (tucked in), and a baseball cap. He was not concerned about the heat, as he had grown up in a village in Durango, Mexico, and spent his youth working outdoors in fields picking crops and shepherding goats under a harsh sun. Between that and his time crossing into the US without authorization by walking through the Chihuahua Desert for several days, or his time spent in Florida picking crops in the summer, little other than the hottest dog days would give him pause to consider the heat. I began working with him when I was 14, and in the ensuing 12 years of work I can count on one hand the number of times we stopped because of the heat.

Even the pain of sunburn was barely worth his acknowledgment. A few years after this particular summer day, my father was accidentally struck in the head by a coworker who was carrying a piece of lumber, causing his scalp to split open. One of the men on the crew, a veteran of the Mexican military who served as a medic, managed to clean the wound and glue the scalp back shut. Dad waited long enough for the glue to dry before continuing to work the rest of the day, undoubtedly bothered by the time lost from the ordeal. My father is mestizo, a colonial term used to describe those that are racially mixed with Native Mexican and European ancestry. While people like my dad are detribalized, possessing no official affiliation to an Indigenous tribe, they are raised with the understanding that they come from the original peoples of the Americas. To me, stories about my dad being seriously injured and still pushing forward with a task, and there are quite a few, are just more proof that the Spanish were never going to completely eradicate the Indigenous Peoples of Mexico. The Spanish made war with the Native Mexicans, worked them to death through slavery and debt bondage, and used the racial hierarchy called the *casta* (caste) system to keep them impoverished and close to death's door, and yet they have persisted.

This particular summer day my job is to make sure that dad has enough shingles, so I scale the ladder periodically with 70lb bundles and try to keep my balance while moving quickly enough to not fall behind. The sound of dad's nail gun firing as he fastens each shingle creates a rhythm; a noticeably fast one since he likes to use a nail gun that lacks a safety mechanism which would require pressing the nose of the tool against the target surface before the trigger can be pulled. He claims that working without the safety feature lets him move faster. If I move fast enough, I can stack up a few bundles of shingles before he can use them up, and buy myself some time to take a break. It is during one of these breaks that dad does something unusual: he talks, but not about the job.

Sitting on his knees, he sits up and removes his cap, running a dark, clay brown hand over his face to wipe away the sweat and then through his black hair. He and I are the only people in our immediate family with black hair. None of his other children, my younger siblings, have the same color hair, which is a bit funny since he and I do not share DNA. My black hair and lighter brown skin come from my birth father, who is from the same region of Mexico, but that is a story for later.

Dad looks at me and it is a little tough to keep eye contact. He has seldom been unkind and has rarely spoken harshly to me, especially at this point in my life. He has never even threatened corporal punishment when I stepped out of line, and cultural standards (whether his culture or my mother's) would have deemed it acceptable. Yet he is an intimidating man. I often think of my dad as being more solid than the ground he walks on, and that sort of presence can be difficult to deal with directly. It certainly was for me at that time. It does not help that he has a scar running across his forehead, over his left eye, that makes it seem like he has a permanent scowl; a trophy awarded to him for surviving a car crash when he was young and fell asleep at the wheel, only to wake up as the car drove off a bridge and into a deep river.

"You're old enough now that if you want to quit school, you can," he says, plainly. "But if you do, you'll come to work with me. That is your choice." And then, without further conversation or concern for a reply, he goes back to nailing shingles. At 16 years old, I had no idea what I wanted to do with my life, but I did know one thing for certain: roofing sucked. And if going to class meant doing less work like this, then the choice was clear.

The purpose of this narrative, as with the other stories that I will share throughout this book, is twofold. The first is to frame the chapter relative to the subject matter. Stories like this thematically connect to the core idea of each chapter in a way that serves the overall function of this book, which is an exploration of the role that mass media played in the formation of my Latino, and specifically Mexican, identity. To discuss identity construction, you will need to know about the identity being constructed. I want to make clear that I am not universalizing my experience; my complicated relationship with the media will resonate with some but not with others. Many of the mass-mediated representations of *Latinidad* that I consumed fostered a sense of shame about being Mexican American which developed into internalized racism. This prompted my desire to move closer to whiteness (the mainstream ideology, not to be confused with the related but distinct ethnic White American Southern identity of my mother's side) in my youth, a choice that left me feeling hollow and that

I have worked to recover from for more than a decade as of this writing. I do not mean to suggest that this is the inevitable experience of every person of Latin American descent who engages with US media. Rather, I share my own story to ground this book in a lived experience, to put a face to this phenomenon.

The second purpose of sharing personal stories is to add texture and detail to a discussion that often lends itself to the abstract and can be difficult to conceptualize concretely. We can address foundational elements of identity construction like whiteness, ideology, and otherness in broad terms, but doing so without examples of real-world manifestations hinders the utility of these conversations and thus limits our ability to grapple with these ideas in a meaningful way.

At its core, this book is about Latinx identity, so we will begin with an operationalization of the concept of *Latinidad*. In a strict sense, the term means "Latinness" and is applied to those whose identities and ancestral origins are rooted, at least in part, in Latin America. The idea of Latinness as an identity positions the concept as a quality that is possessed and measures authenticity because to have an identity means meeting certain criteria, and this is where we encounter our first patch of difficult terrain that we will need to navigate. The existence of a single term that encapsulates all of the countries from Mexico to Argentina and Chile and the surrounding islands, and the corresponding application of the concept of *Latinidad* to the myriad communities and peoples within or associated with those countries is intrinsically reductive. Doing so places these complex, multidimensional identities into a discrete category without regard for physical, cultural, or social borders; systemic tensions; histories of oppression; areas of overlap and divergence; cultural diffusion; and power dynamics. So, rather than conceptualizing *Latinidad* as a fixed and rigid category of identity, it would be more productive to consider it as an umbrella term for identities of particularity, one where the borders of that conceptual space are porous and blurred. By this I mean that *Latinidad* is socially constructed in a variety of contexts that are unified by some basic sociocultural themes, while also engaging in a both/and form of identity construction rather than an either/or paradigm (Gonzalez, Chavez, and Englebrecht, 2014). It is a vernacular identity constituted in a moment in time as a part of a continual chain of ancestry. My father is neither Latino nor Indigenous; he is both as they exist in that contentious conceptual space of *mestizaje*, of being racially and culturally mixed with Indigenous and Spanish ancestry. I am not Chicano *or* a Southerner from America; I am both, a Latino in the New South. My children are not White *or* Latina; they are the next link in the diasporic chain, and will exist at the intersection of the power associated with the privileges of their skin color and the modification of that privilege that comes from an ethnic identity which was carried on the back of their *abuelo* (grandfather) as he swam the Rio Bravo. *Latinidad* is not a box to check on a form, nor is it a standard against which to be measured. It is a paint palette where the colors of the past mix with the colors of the present to create something new. Ultimately this means that my *Latinidad*, informed by *Mexicanidad* (Mexican identity) and American Southern whiteness and distilled into a Chicano identity contextualized in the New South, is a sutured identity; an identity that exists within the broader, dynamic context of history and the contemporary moment (Hall, 1990).

Another area of difficult terrain that we must traverse is that of race as it pertains to being Latinx. Race is a social construct, which is to say that it is a human-made concept for organizing peoples into groups. In this case, those categories correspond to physical appearance, and yet there is no biological component to race (Omi and Winant, 2015). Strictly speaking, there is no Latinx race. Latinx people belong to a variety of these social categories; some are White, Black, Brown, and so forth. However, in contemporary society in the United States, one way in which we are racialized is through mass media representations. Racialization is the process through which we become incorporated into a racial hierarchy to fit an existing and ongoing racial regime through a variety of mechanisms such as behaviors, traditions, cultural affecta- tions, and so on, which ultimately leads to the reproduction of the society's structure of racial domination (Bonilla-Silva, 2015). As I discuss throughout this book, Latinx people are racialized through a range of mass media texts and sites that reinforce a social structure that distances *Latinidad* from whiteness as a racial identity even for those who present an outward appearance of whiteness. A central aspect of this process of racialization is that historically we have not represented ourselves; rather, we have had ourselves represented to us. In his essay "Cultural Identity and Diaspora," Stuart Hall (1990) addresses this phenomenon in the context of the African diaspora in the Caribbean and media representation. He writes,

> Where Africa was a case of the unspoken, Europe was
> a case of that which is endlessly speaking - and end-
> lessly speaking us. The European presence interrupts
> the innocence of the whole discourse of "difference" in

the Caribbean by introducing the question of power. "Europe" belongs irrevocably to the play of power, to the lines of force and consent, to the role of the dominant, in Caribbean culture. In terms of colonialism, underdevelopment, poverty and the racism of colour, the European presence is that which, in visual representation, has positioned the black subject within its dominant regimes of representation: the colonial discourse, the literatures of adventure and exploration, the romance of the exotic, the ethnographic and travelling eye, the tropical languages of tourism, travel brochure and Hollywood and the violent, pornographic languages of ganja and urban violence. (Hall, 1990, p. 232–233)

Hall's characterization of Europe "speaking" Caribbean identity and thus constructing it in ways that are exotic, violent, and vulgar and racially inferior could be easily mapped onto the relationship between the United States and *Latinidad*. One salient example of this is through news discourse related to immigration, wherein the phenomenon of migration from Latin America to the United States is heavily associated with dangerous, foreign Brown bodies, to the point that the concepts become seemingly intrinsically linked (Heuman and Gonzalez, 2018). This is to say, to identify as Latinx is to be associated with a Brown body and thus racialized downward in the context of a racial hierarchy (Bonilla-Silva, 2015). Mass media depictions of people with the same skin color as my father become strategic representations of all Latinx people, and thus situate them in America's racial hierarchy. In the case of people who do not fit this physical description, to be identified as Latinx is to be at the least ethnically othered, to be seen as non-American, non-normative (read: not-White-enough). This, along with the ethnicization of labor, and instances like that day of working on the roof with my father, become more than a man teaching his son a skill (Brayton, 2011). Those moments become racialized in a way that pushes me further toward *Latinidad* and away from whiteness.

With that in mind, let us discuss my academic toolbox. I am the son of a carpenter, and for over a decade worked with my father on job sites remodeling homes or building them from the foundation up. My dad did not really have a specialty in the sense of having one specific element of construction that he focused on because he did everything. From doing framing and roofing to hanging drywall, doing tiling, and painting, he could do just about every aspect of home construction, and I was right there alongside him until I was 26 years old. This generalist approach to working helped him to stay busy and also afforded him the chance to learn new skills and techniques. My dad's formal education ended in the sixth grade when he had to go to work full-time to help support his family, but he is a life-long learner. My perspective on academia and research closely mirrors, and was likely informed by, my father's attitude toward his profession. I like to think of concepts, theories, and methodologies as tools in a toolbox, like the tools my dad carries in the back of his work van. Every theory, conceptual framework, and scholastic orientation has strengths and limitations. Each is made to answer different sorts of questions to varying degrees of depth and complexity. And just as no one tool can do everything needed to build a home, no one theory or concept can provide a comprehensive understanding of how society functions in the creation of identity. So, in order to build this house, or to engage with the subject of identity, let us take a look at the tools that we will be using.

The first and perhaps most important concept for this book is that of *nepantla*. *Nepantla*, as used by Gloria Anzaldua (2012), refers to a state of liminality, a territory caught in between two or more forces that pull us in different directions. It is a metaphysical border between worlds that those under the umbrella of *Latinidad* have to navigate in perpetuity due to the larger sociocultural and political forces that have shaped our lives and histories. The saying "we didn't cross the border, the border crossed us," often associated with the Chicano movement (Cisneros, 2013), still rings true as a commentary on the artificiality of the oppressive international and colonial forces that have shaped Latinx communities. I contend that it would also be accurate to say now that we *are* the borders, as our identities function as contested sites of nepantilism.

Working on the roof with my father that day is an example of those metaphysical borders that reside within us. In the hours that we spent on the roof, several phenomena occurred. An immigrant father was teaching his American-born son knowledge that would be useful for survival. This type of labor, working outdoors with hands and hardware, had been how my father survived in Mexico. This was also the transference of cultural knowledge that defined his identity in terms of his race, his class, and his gender; a dark-skinned mestizo (mixed Native Mexican and European), a *campesino* (peasant farmer), and a *ranchero* (rugged, rural masculine man). In my father's world, men work, and men like him work outside with their backs bent. On that day and many others, we represented a negotiation between two very different worlds. I may be mestizo, but I am light-skinned enough that there is always a chance I will be seen as White. I have at times lived within the categories of the working poor and the working class, but I have no point of reference for *campesino* life. I have always thought of myself as a man, but a *ranchero*? Never. To be a *ranchero* in the style of the men in my family required a degree of confidence I did not have at that point, and even when I developed the confidence, I never invested enough pride in the manifestations of my masculinity to see myself as that kind of ruggedly masculine man. But bridging the boundaries between these two worlds, this space of nepantilism, was labor, that is, labor as an expression of identity; labor as a ritual anchored in tradition; labor as a heritage that transcends geopolitical borders, generations, and racial status. And as I learned this type of labor from my father over the years, I did so against a backdrop of mass media that reduced *Latinidad* in general and *Mexicanidad* in particular to a handful of stereotypes that included chief among them, that of the manual laborer (Brayton, 2011). People like my father have historically been fetishized for their perceived capacity for doing extremely arduous work, and pop culture depictions of that stereotype have solidified that perception to the point of being common sense. If there is hard work to be done and quickly, you hire Mexicans. The fresher, that is to say, the more recently arrived in the country, the better. Thus, microlevel moments of interpersonal engagement become imbued with a racialized, decidedly white supremacist, ideology.

Moments like this, whether regarding labor, education, familial relationships, or any other aspects of life, are sites of struggle between intersecting boundaries. In my case I am, have been, and will be, torn between the worlds of my imagined ancestral homes of rural Durango, Mexico, and the countryside of central North Carolina. I am the border where two worlds connect., One world is that of detribalized natives and mestizo peasants who were remixed into the silhouette of a *ranchero* wearing ostrich skin cowboy boots for danc-ing and a wide brim sombrero meant to block out the sun while working in a field. tThe other world is that of cast-off Celts and other European laborers who carved out a home in the American South as a part of the British colonial project, occupying land stolen from the Indigenous Peoples of the region. Those roughnecks often maligned as White trash have historically operated as the boots of empire: used to expand Manifest Destiny and stomp out opposition, only to then be discarded without care or concern once they were too broken and damaged to be of use. These are two of the worlds that have created the *nepantla* where I find myself.

Yet, whereas my Americanness has been nourished, my *Latinidad* has often either been starved or fed rancid food—at times by others and at times by me, which has led to the need for con-structing and reconstructing my *Latinidad* over the years. My negotiation of nepantilism has been largely informed by the mass media and racial ideologies that have permeated daily life. Ideologies about what it means to be normal (read: White), to be a racialized "other," and depictions of "good" and "bad" Mexicans, dangerous immigrants, and respectable Americans have consti-tuted the media ecosystem.

The following tools in my academic toolbox will help you to understand how mass media and racial ideologies have operated in concert with each other:

- social constructionism
- ideology
- discourse
- articulation
- racial formation
- whiteness
- otherness
- narrative paradigm
- suturing

At its core, social constructionism is the idea that reality is defined socially and that those definitions are made manifest materially (Guess, 2006). By this I mean that when two or more individuals interact, they construct a reality between them, and the consequences of that reality are dependent on the actions of the individuals. For example, if I introduce myself by saying, "Hi, my name is Gabe," I am attempting to create a social reality with another person wherein we are peers. However, if I introduce myself by saying, "Hi, I'm Dr. Cruz," then I have modified the power dynamic of the interaction by inserting an honorific signifying my education while withholding my first name, which in effect makes the interaction more formal and perhaps even makes the power dynamic asymmetrical in my favor depending on the context. Furthermore, if I introduce myself by saying, "*Hola, me llamo* Gabriel Cruz" with a Spanish-language inflection in my pronunciation, then I am signifying my *Latinidad* in that social interaction. Each one of these phrases has implications for how the other person will react and will thus impact our relationship and by extension material reality. When the ways in which we are socialized on an individual level are normalized through widespread practice and passed on to the next generation, then these social constructions of reality become legitimized and institutionalized, creating social order (Guess, 2006).

If we understand social construction at the individual level as the interpersonal creation of a social reality, then we must consider the implications at a grand scale, and this is where we encounter the concept of ideology and its relationship with mass media. An ideology is a framework for understanding and organizing social reality; in doing so, ideologies create cohesion within a society but can also cause struggle (Loomba, 2005). One useful way to think about ideology is as a means of producing hegemony. Hegemony, a term coined by the Italian communist party leader and organizer Antonio Gramsci, is the idea of power that is created through force and consent that is wielded by those who have access to the force and means of facilitating consent. Essentially,

> the ruling classes achieve domination not by force or coercion alone, but also by creating subjects who "willingly" submit to being ruled. Ideology is crucial in creating consent, it is the medium through which certain ideas are transmitted and, more important, held to be true. (Loomba, 2005, p. 30)

Ideology and the social construction of reality are enmeshed as each informs the other. Through socialization, we adopt

perceptions of what is and is not normative based on the ideologies we are exposed to; and at the same time, we recreate,
modify, or subvert a given ideology by creating social realities
that are either compatible with or in opposition to those ideologies. In a narrow sense, this could manifest as embracing the
"traditional" way of life embodied by your parents or as rejecting
it entirely. Both choices involve creating a social reality, and there
is no neutral position to take. The process of being socialized into
a particular ideology is a complex process involving factors such
as, but not limited to, community influence, social networks,
institutional affiliation and participation, and mass media consumption. For the purposes of this book, I will focus on the role
of mass media as a vehicle for ideologies. Through mass media,
ideological messages are disseminated to the public with varying degrees of success in terms of reach and internalization by
audiences. Whether through television, film, music, news broadcasts, or literature, every piece of media contains elements of
ideological frameworks that advance a given worldview. This is
not inherently positive or negative; rather, it is merely the nature
of human endeavors to convey information, and as such these
messages are not value neutral. Every piece of media reinforces,
modifies, or subverts an ideology, and in order to understand
how that happens, we must consider the function of discourse.

Discourse is intimately connected to the creation and maintenance of a given ideology. In this context, discourse does not
merely refer to conversation, whether written or spoken, but to
the multitude of ways that we communicate on an individual and
mass-mediated scale. Spoken words, written language, pictures,
music, film, painted portraits, everything that communicates

engages in discourse relative to a given subject matter. From this perspective, we must also understand that discourse is intrinsically related to power because the ability to create discourse indicates a degree of sociocultural, political, or economic power. Through communication, power is exerted by individuals and institutions to shape social reality; thus, those with the influence to do so are imbuing with their own ideologies, the tools we use to engage with reality (Kinefuchi and Cruz, 2015). In terms of mass-mediated discourse, we should consider the role of media producers such as news organizations and film studios. Through a combination of language, visual communication, narrative construction, and sound the producers of mass media frame reality in ways that are informed by and reproduce ideologies, such as the idea that poor and non-White residents of a town devastated by natural disaster are dangerous and inclined toward criminality as they struggle to survive (Lacy and Haspel, 2011), or that the violence of aggrieved White men is not only normative but also morally justifiable and heroic (Cramer, Cruz, and Donofrio, 2023). Referring to my experience of working on the roof with my father, the discourse of labor in the United States is often racialized as *Mexicanidad* and is closely associated with physical labor such as construction or agricultural work (Brayton, 2011); and while a Mexican identity is a matter of nationality rather than race, the popular culture representations of Mexican identity have been historically associated with Brown bodies (Heuman and Gonzalez, 2018). Thus, the process of working with my father and learning this type of labor supports the construction of a racialized identity, not because my father sought to pass on his brownness, but because the skills he had learned and decided to pass on were imbued with a racial quality by dominant mass-mediated discourse.

When the process of articulation, which creates a unity of multiple elements that are not intrinsically linked, (Hall, 2019), and the discursive construction of reality produce understandings about race and racialized identities within a given societal context, such as the United States, then race-making is taking place. This practice of creating racialized identities, whether through mass-mediated articulations, government policy, the praxis of social movements, or interpersonal actions, leads to the development of racial formations. A racial formation can be understood as the "process by which racial identities are created, lived out, transformed, and destroyed" (Omi and Winant, 2015, p. 109). This characterization of the phenomenon emphasizes the fluidity and pervasiveness of racial ideologies in a way that cannot be overstated. The race-making process occurs at the microlevel with individual expressions of racial identity and interpersonal experiences of racial solidarity or discrimination, as well as at the macrolevel through mass-mediated discourse evident in popular culture artifacts and news media. Within the context of the United States, racialized identities such as blackness or brownness and ethnic identities such as *Latinidad* are constructed relative to whiteness. The racial formation of whiteness is dynamic, fluid, and constantly evolves in order to maintain its hegemonic position, thus making it difficult to pin down in concrete terms. Therefore, for the purpose of this text and to operationalize the idea in a pragmatic manner, I assert that we should understand whiteness as a racial ideology that is constructed through discourse to be invisible, neutral, and central to society. In their foundational article "Whiteness: A Strategic Rhetoric," Thomas Nakayama and Robert Krizek (1995) articulate six strategies used to socially construct whiteness as a racial formation:

- The association of whiteness with power and status by virtue of being a member of the majority population.
- Defining whiteness as the lack of any other racial or ethnic identity, thus making it seem to be the default identity as well as a non-color-oriented identity.
- The naturalization of whiteness as a scientific classification that describes a person superficially without social or historical context.
- The territorialization of whiteness by binding it to a national border, in this case the United States. Thus, to be White is to be assumed as American, whereas being non-White carries the implication of being non-American.
- The rejection of whiteness as a label at all, and instead only identifying as American as an attempt to avoid terms that could cause social division. This in turn obscures the role of race in society while attempting to create unity under a national identity that is already heavily associated with whiteness.
- The association of White identity with Europe broadly or specific European countries in a way that positions the identity as an accessory to one's life but not defining in a meaningful way.

What is most important to understand about these rhetorical strategies for the racial formation of whiteness, relative to the premise of this text, is that by occupying a position of normalcy, centrality, and invisibility, all other racial and ethnic identities are constructed as deficient, marginal, and aberrant. *Latinidad* is no exception to this rule. Across the various types of media, whether news, political discourse, or popular culture, *Latinidad* has been constructed as a category of "others," racially, ethnically, and socially. From public discourse descriptions of Latin American immigrants as animals (Santa Ana, 2013) and pollution (Cisneros, 2008) to popular fiction framing us as criminals (Mastro, Behm-Morawitz, and Ortiz, 2007), we have been consistently constructed as existential threats to the United States despite many of our communities having roots in this landmass that predate this nation.

The American system of mass media has historically served as a vital vehicle for the dissemination of white supremacist ideologies and the maintenance of centuries-long racial formations. However, American mass media is not monolithic and operates as a contested space where prosocial ideologies of race and justice continue to wage an uphill battle. Latinxs like myself who find themselves having to navigate this mass-mediated terrain are bombarded with dehumanizing as well as dimensionally prosocial messages, each attempting to draw us into a particular ideological system for co-constructing reality. A key tool in my academic toolbox, one that I learned the basics of intuitively before I ever entered the world of higher education, is that of the narrative paradigm, and it has been crucial in my navigation of the mass-media landscape. At its core, the narrative paradigm asserts that humans are story-telling creatures that construct social reality through narratives which are told time and again (Atkinson and Calafell, 2009). Over time, these narratives are propagated throughout society and eventually coalesce into pervasive discursive formations and ideologies that social-ize new members of society and normalize perspectives and modes of being (Atkinson and Calafell, 2009). The reason I say that I learned the basics of this concept early in my life is because I, like most people, learned to make sense of the world through stories. I learned to identify with narratives featuring characters who, like me, possessed identities that were considered non-normative. I learned to buy into ideologies that facilitated inter-nalized racism through mass-mediated images of faceless Brown immigrants from Latin America who, if cable news pundits were to be believed, placed the United States on the precipice of col-lapse. Through mass media narratives, I learned how to increase my proximity to whiteness, both as a matter of survival and as an attempt to escape my own racial trauma.

And this is where we come to the final tool in our academic tool-box: suturing a cultural identity. In the essay "Cultural Identity and Diaspora," Hall (1990) posits two positions for understanding cul-tural identity relative to diasporic populations. The first position is that cultural identity is a matter of uncovering that which was taken away by colonization in order to rediscover an identity that is essential, fixed, and eternal, something that fills the gap left by colonization (Hall, 1990). However, it is the second position for understanding cultural identity that is useful for inclusion in our academic toolbox. He writes,

> Cultural identity, in this second sense, is a matter of "becoming" as well as "being." It belongs to the future as much as to the past. It is not something which already exists, transcending place, time, history, and culture. Cultural identities come from somewhere, have

histories. But like everything which is historical, they undergo constant transformation. Far from being eternally fixed in some essentialised past, they are subject to the continuous "play" of history, culture, and power. Far from being grounded in a mere "recovery" of the past, which is waiting to be found, and which when found, will secure our sense of ourselves in eternity, identities are the names we give to the different ways we are positioned by, and position ourselves within, the narratives of the past. (Hall, 1990, p. 225)

Hall (1990) describes the construction of a cultural identity from this perspective as a suture or an unstable point of identification made from a position within the context of history, time, and place. I use the language of suturing a cultural identity because I find it operates as an appropriate metaphor for this process of constructing *Latinidad*. At the beginning of this chapter, I addressed how it is better to think of *Latinidad* as an umbrella term for a set of identities of particularity rather than a rigid categorization used to measure Latinness. One of the qualities that characterizes these identities of particularity is a common history of the wound of colonization in Latin America (Lopez, 2018). This is not to say that all Latinxs have been wounded by colonization in the same way. Different communities, and indeed different individuals, relate to colonization and its legacy in unique ways. My assertion is that colonization itself was a wound, one that continues to bleed, that has impacted every person and community which is positioned within *Latinidad*. In the following chapters of this book, I will explore that wound's manifestation in US mass media from the macrosocial and microindividual levels and discuss the ways in which I have attempted to heal it by suturing it closed, creating a Latino identity for myself that at times has included the use of mass media.

The premise of this book is the construction of *Latinidad* using mass media, and in the following chapters I will discuss the role that mass media played in my life as I constructed an identity informed by racialized *Latinidad* and structural whiteness. In this first chapter, I have laid out the conceptual and theoretical underpinnings that will be important to understand in order to get the most out of the rest of the chapters. I refer to this collection of concepts as my academic toolbox and these tools will be necessary for the work ahead.

In chapter 2, I set the context for the society I was born into, how my journey of racialization began, and why I came to depend on mass-mediated *Latinidad* for my identity construction. I describe the Latinx community that I initially grew up in and its uneasy relationship with the local American community. I also touch on the broader national context that shaped the world I was entering when I left the small town of Siler City, North Carolina.

In chapter 3, I discuss *Latinidad* as it is constructed through that reality-defining institution we call the US news media. I address how Latinx communities are framed through the use of negative stereotypes such as criminality, invasion, and as a societal burden. I also illustrate how attempts at positive framing often do more harm than good, shifting from describing Latinx people as being criminals to being objects of pity devoid of agency and in need of charity.

In chapter 4, I engage with the great epistemological tools of fictional television and film. Specifically, I address how *Latinidad* is constructed in those formats in a way that relies on tropes, stereotypes, and archetypes to neatly package and commodify *Latinidad* for historically non-Latinx audiences. I also discuss some examples of texts that resist the entrenched norms and patterns of dehumanizing representation.

In chapter 5, I focus on a particular kind of fiction that is near to my heart and ripe for analysis: superhero narratives. I discuss the often fraught but occasionally productive relationship between *Latinidad* and superhero stories both in terms of comics/sequential art narratives and their adaptations to television and film. I also engage with the theme of symbolic otherness that is a staple in superhero narratives and the role it serves in trying to fill the gap created by the lack of adequate representation of *Latinidad* in these sorts of stories.

In chapter 6, I engage with a medium that has at times served as the most important form of entertainment in my life, and thus played a crucial role in my self-concept: video games. Video games are unique as a mediated form of entertainment as compared to the news, television, film, and so on due to the participatory nature of the medium, which allows players to construct the narrative along with the game with varying degrees of agency. As such, this medium allows players to enact an identity rather than strictly consume that identity as presented to them by the producers of the text. It is only appropriate then, as a lifelong gamer, to include a discussion of *Latinidad* as it has been made manifest within this type of media.

In chapter 7, I conclude the book by addressing several key themes that have run throughout this volume including: the value of Latinx identity, a reflection on my own process of racialization through mass media, and how to move forward in such a fluidly defined territory. I discuss the utility of *Latinidad*, where I perceive that it falls short in its functionality with regard to media, and offer tools for Latinx-identifying people for navigating their own process of racialization through mass media.

2
An exodus and an exigence

My mom has an old .38. It is a five-round, snub-nosed revolver made by Rossi, and if you ask her if she is carrying it, the most concrete answer you will get is "maybe." But there was a time when she wore it openly, displayed for all the world to see on a shoulder holster. In her youth it served as a declaration to anyone curious that she did not have any problems, only solutions. But these days, more than anything else, it is a relic of the past and a reminder of where we come from, she and I.

It is the summer of 1992 in the small southern town of Siler City, North Carolina. A small business with the name Tienda Gabriel written in big, pink letters painted across huge windows, is open. When you walk through the front door of the business, you can see that the building is divided into two sections, a grocery store on the left and a restaurant on the right. On the grocery side, the smell of refrigeration and the hum of cold storage units is constant, along with the intermingling scents of ground-up shrimp seasoning, dried guajillo chiles, and a host of other spices. On the other side of the store, where the restaurant is located, the air is filled with the smell of tacos de *lengua*, *milanesa* de pollo, cilantro, and a variety of other aromas. It is noon on a Friday in the summer and the store is busy. A corrido by Los Tigres Del Norte struts through the store, soon to be followed by a crooning ballad by Juan Gabriel. The store is populated with Latinas shopping for groceries, and Latinos eating at the dining counter and in booths for their lunch breaks. Doña Rita, a Mexican woman in her mid-40s, is about her business in the kitchen cooking food that the American Medical Association might not exactly consider healthy but is certainly good for you when what you need is a taste of the home that you left behind in Mexico. Luis, a young man from the Mexican state of Nayarit, and Doña Rita's son, is on his lunch break from his job at the local lumberyard. He is barely into his adulthood, but he and his brothers, who are also sitting at the lunch counter, do the labor of grown, mature men. Esther, a recently immigrated Mexican girl in her senior year of high school, flits quickly between customers and the kitchen, taking orders, pouring drinks, and serving food. One of the customers at the counter seems a bit out of place among the young, Brown men wolfing down their lunches in a hurry to not be late getting back to the lumberyard. Bill is fair-skinned with exceedingly pale, blue eyes that shine with the same vigor and charisma he had when he was 20, even though he is a little more than twice that age. He chats with Esther when she comes by to check on him; his Spanish is as effortlessly fluent as his primary language, English, although he does have to catch himself from slipping into Arabic once in a while. Unlike the young men, he is taking his time. He is waiting for the store to slow down so that he can speak to the owner about a work-related project. Bill is an immigrant advocate; he helps people navigate the immigration system regardless of their legal status and he knows that this store presents an opportunity for better engaging the local immigrant community.

In a booth toward the back of the restaurant sits a middle-aged, red-headed, on-duty police officer eating a torta. If his uniform did not mark him as an outsider in this particular space, his white skin surely would. He appears to be minding his business, but he is paying close attention to his surroundings and in particular to the front door of the store, which is in plain view from his seat. The officer notes the dark-skinned men, but they are not who he is watching for. He is confident that they do not have papers to be in this country but that is not his concern; he is watching for other White men, the kind that wear denim jackets with rebel flag patches sewn onto them. The kind of men who have been vocal about their displeasure with this establishment and took matters into their own hands late last year by making an attempt on the life of the proprietress while she was locking up the store. Since then, he had been making regular visits to the store during his lunch break to keep an eye on things and to make his presence known to any more would-be assailants. He knows the owner of the store. She has worked as an interpreter for local law enforcement, emergency services, and the local health department every now and then. He thinks it would be a terrible thing for something to happen to her or the business, since it seems like the Mexicans are here to stay.

At the check-out counter close to the front door, two White American women help several Latinas with their purchases. The older of the two, a blond woman in her early 30s named Nina, rings up the groceries for a woman buying chickpeas for pozole and a bag of Maseca for making tortillas. Nina is all smiles, due in part to her desire to come across as friendly and because of her nervous self-awareness at her functional but elementary Spanish that she speaks with a heavy, local Southern accent. The other woman, a 24-year-old brunette named Bonnie, who owns Tienda Gabriel, is assisting two Mexican women as they respectively scan through the jewelry counter. Bonnie's Spanish is imperfect but competent, and so she converses with the women fairly easily as she pulls out gold earrings for one shopper and a gold bracelet for the other. But what stands out to the women more than Bonnie's Spanish is the revolver in the shoulder strap on her right side. And that is the point, to be noticed. After the attack by members of the local chapter of the Ku Klux Klan, she figured that it would not be enough for her just to carry a weapon; other potential adversaries needed to know that she was carrying. As she places the earrings back into the display case, something catches her eye off to the left toward the grocery section of the store. Something she is always on guard for, forever vigilant. She calls out in a voice with remarkably little of her native North Carolinian accent, "¡Hijo!" The word catches me in the chest, and I stand stock-still with my four-year-old hand in a box of Duvalin Mexican candies with one firmly in my grasp as I consider whether it is worth it to take the candy and run. The choice is easy: it absolutely is.

Dignity and Respect

In 1992, George H. W. Bush was serving his last year as president, the Cold War had been declared officially over, and small, rural towns in the Southern United States like Siler City, North Carolina, were dying. The closing or migration of factory jobs in the 1980s had left many small towns economically devastated and with populations that were getting increasingly older (Cuadros, 2006). The saving grace for Siler City, what helped it keep from plunging further into economic despair, was the local Latinx population. In the mid 1980s, local poultry processing plants began to recruit immigrants from the US-Mexico border to work in the plant, most of whom were young, unmarried men from Mexico; by the 1990s, women and children would also begin settling into the community (Cravey, 1997). This influx of laborers who were trafficked into Siler City created a migration phenomenon that, whether directly or indirectly, brought many people significant to me into my life. My birth father, Sotero, came from Mexico to work in a poultry plant, where he met my mother. Within two years of first meeting, they courted, got married, and had me. That marriage was short-lived and before I was five years old, Sotero was out of my life almost completely. Oddly enough, my dad, Baltazar, also came to Siler City to find work around the same time. But even though he and my mother knew some of the same people, they did not know each other. In fact, she and I left Siler City in 1996 to move to Manassas, Virginia, and we would not meet the man I would learn to call my father until early 2000 after having moved back to North Carolina. My eventual godparents of confirmation, Esther and Luis, also entered my life during my early days of living in Siler City. They had not come to town to work in the poultry plants; rather, they had made their respective ways to town following rather circuitous routes from Nayarit, Mexico to California and then ultimately North Carolina. Like many other people, they had come because they knew people who worked in Siler City.

Tienda Gabriel served as a location for the nascent Latin American community that was taking shape, for whom spaces of belonging were few and far between. The store became a hub for the immigrant community in general and the Mexican immigrant community in particular as the products and food sold in the store were typically associated with or were directly from Mexico, a conscious choice made by my mom since it seemed that the majority of the immigrants came from Mexico and because the Mexican community was her primary point of reference for Latin Americans at the time. Over time the store grew, not just in terms of its popularity but also its visibility and role in shaping the community. The store went from just selling groceries and household products to including the restaurant, and later to offering translation services for medical, legal, and business documents. Bill McFadden, a local immigrant advocate who would later become my godfather of baptism, used the store to engage in outreach with the immigrant community and connect people who needed help with a local organization that specialized in offering support to local families. As a result, Tienda Gabriel went from being a place where needs were met to a place where problems could be solved, and in doing so it became a valuable part of helping the Latinx immigrants establish roots in the community.

Beyond being a place of business, Tienda Gabriel was also its own cultural space, a social construct that existed in stark contrast to the local community and the prevailing national sentiment toward Latin American immigrants. Specifically, the store was characterized by the discourse of Mexican popular culture and the different dialects of Mexican Spanish spoken by the clientele, as well as the owner, who learned through conversations and by consuming media. The visual rhetoric and symbolism of advertisements for local Mexican bands, sarapes and piñatas hanging in the store for sale, CDs by Mexican musicians on display, and the presence of racialized Latinx bodies conversing, laughing, and going about their business created an atmosphere that marked the space as racially and ethnically distinct from the rest of Siler City. According to official US census data, in 1990 there were 184 people of Hispanic origin, 3,393 White Americans, and 1,293 Black Americans in the town limits of Siler City (US Department of Commerce, 1990). Even operating with the understanding that the figure for the identified Hispanic community is likely an undercount, since immigrants who lack the appropriate authorization to live in the United States may be inclined to avoid census agents and efforts to gather accurate information, the difference in population size is clear and the businesses in the area reflect the demographics of the time. Tienda Gabriel was an island of *Latinidad* in an ocean of southeastern whiteness.

Within the national context, the political discourse around Latin American immigration had become a particularly heated subject by the mid-1990s. The regulation of the US-Mexico border, and those who cross it, has been a significant issue within the United States since 1848 when the United States colonized northern Mexico as a part of its Manifest Destiny-fueled westward expansion. Since then, the United States has grappled with how to control Americans of Mexican descent as well as Mexicans and other Latin Americans who have sought to enter the United States through the southern border. Since 1848, the United States has attempted to use immigration quotas (US

Department of State, n.d.), lynchings (Carrigan and Webb, 2003), sterilization (Novak et al., 2018), and ethnic cleansing through mass deportation (Fernandez, 2014), among other strategies to subjugate those with roots in Latin America. In the 1990s, these efforts by the United States came in the form of legislation like California Proposition 187 and the Clinton administration's policy of prevention through deterrence. Proposition 187, also referred to as the Save Our State referendum, was a ballot initiative that

> restricted undocumented immigrants from the state's public services, including access to public education and healthcare. In addition, the proposition directed teachers and healthcare professionals to report any individuals suspected of being undocumented to the Immigration and Naturalization Services (INS) or the California Attorney General. (Library of Congress, n.d.)

The initiative passed with 59 percent of voters in favor of the measure (Library of Congress, n.d.). Within weeks of the policy being passed, a federal judge issued an injunction against the legislation and it was ultimately ruled unconstitutional in 1998; in 2004, a similar referendum was proposed but did not pass. In response to the kind of social and political outrage that prompted the creation of California Proposition 187, the Clinton administration enacted the policy of "prevention through deterrence," which attempted to make the journey into the United States exceedingly difficult in order to reduce immigration. The policy was adopted in 1994 and explicitly sought to deter irregular border crossing by "disrupt[ing] […] traditional entry and smuggling routes" so migrants would be "forced over" more "hostile terrain" far away from populated areas where those at risk of death by exposure to harsh elements might be able to seek help. Immediately, the number of border deaths nearly tripled. Prevention through Deterrence has contributed to at least 10,000 deaths at the border over the last three decades, a number that is certainly an undercount, since Border Patrol systematically fails to properly count deaths and since human remains in remote areas along the border are rapidly scavenged and scattered by the elements and wildlife. (Human Rights Watch, 2023)

Locally, this anti-immigrant sentiment was also vibrant. I referenced in the story at the start of this chapter that my mother carried a firearm, and I alluded to an attack that was made on her and me by a local chapter of the Ku Klux Klan. My mother was known to the Klan before she opened the store because she was one of the few White women in town who had married a Mexican, my birth father. When she opened Tienda Gabriel, she was a young, divorced White woman with a Mexican baby, with high visibility in the community, who was known for making life easier for the local Latinx community; and all of these elements led certain individuals to view her as an easy target for sending a political message to the immigrants and anyone attempting to help them. And so, one evening in the Fall of 1991, three White American men wearing denim jackets with Confederate flags sewn onto them made an attempt on her life.

They came to the restaurant just before closing time and after everyone else had left. My mother was the only person working, and I was in the back of the store in my "office" where I watched cartoons and played my Sega Genesis. The men cornered her in the storefront and told them what they had in mind. They planned on sexually assaulting her before killing her, and had they been successful, and also learned that I was there, I do not doubt they would have killed me as well. But then, whether by luck or divine intervention, something happened: one of my mother's regular customers stopped by. I do not know the gentleman's name, but mom described him as a middle-aged Black man with a cognitive disability who would come by the store regularly to eat and cash his disability check when he received it each month. My mother's store was one of the few places in town where he was accepted since many of the White business owners did not like doing business with Black folks and those who did not discriminate, did not like having him around because he had poor hygiene, likely due to his disability. So, Tienda Gabriel was one of the few places in town where he was treated with dignity and respect. When he walked in and saw that the three men were advancing on my mother, he quickly interjected himself and asked what they were doing and if she was OK. At that moment, the Klansmen decided to leave rather than deal with both my mom and the interloper. That was not the end of the harassment against us, but it was the last time they made such a bold move.

My mother's Aunt Della used to be a waitress at a local Woolworth's during the segregation era and she was often the only waitress who treated the Black customers fairly. Sometimes she was the only one who would wait on them at all. When the other waitresses asked why, she said that "every person is some mother's child," and that was a perspective that she passed on to mom, and that is how my mother ran her business. That approach to interacting with the marginalized very likely saved our lives.

In the Summer of 1996, my mother and I left Siler City for Manassas, Virginia, where my grandparents lived at the time. A couple years prior to leaving town, my mother made a career change. She sold the store to a local Latino businessman and friend named Byron, and she transitioned into working for a community outreach organization that was focused on helping underserved populations including the burgeoning Latinx community. But the change in career did nothing to stop the problems that prompted us to move. The Klan continued to harass us and mom still had to deal with the virulent machismo within the Latinx community that resulted in men treating her as an inferior even as she tried to help their families. Having earned a reputation as someone who could help the vulnerable meant that she was often approached by people who needed what few resources she could spare. Once, a high school-age Latina showed up at our home at 2 a.m. asking for help. Her family had discovered that she was queer and kicked her out of the house. She did not know mom except by reputation and so asked her for help. Mom gave her a place to stay and then helped her get to another family member's home the next day. While mom was happy to help, the realization that people who did not know her knew where she lived was unsettling, particularly since some people meant her harm. On top of all of these difficulties, my mother learned that some of those she had thought would be allies, turned out to be enemies. Several scholars from a local university at the time had come to Siler City to research the Latinx community and began to frame my mother as a grifter who was taking advantage of the immigrants. They accused this single mother of taking financial advantage of the immigrants for charging for translation services. The fact that she did so at a fraction of the cost charged by lawyers made no difference to them. In their estimation, she should have provided those services for free and to do otherwise was unethical. All of these factors combined with the interpersonal fallout and baggage from my parents' messy divorce prompted us to leave and attempt to start over in an entirely new context.

Living in Siler City was the last time I would live among a Latinx community in my day-to-day life, and so the development of my *Latinidad*, the process of my racialization, changed dramatically. Over the next 20+ years, I occupied different levels of economic status, but the spaces in which I operated were almost always defined by whiteness. By this I mean that the social structures, such as the education system and houses of worship, were almost always those that were created to serve mainstream White American needs; indeed, the people in these spaces were almost always White Americans. Exchanging a Latinx community for White communities that were heavily shaped by anti-immigrant and anti-Latinx political rhetoric, and having been left behind by my Latino father, meant that I had to turn elsewhere to develop a sense of *Latinidad*: the media. In the following chapters I discuss how the news, fictional television shows, film, and superhero comics have informed my racialization and the development of my *Latinidad*.

3
Dirty (digital) Mexicans

Walk with me for a moment through some old memories.

It is a summer morning in 2000 and I am at the Boys & Girls Club in Sanford, North Carolina, waiting with a bunch of other 11- and 12-year-old kids in a classroom for a counselor to start the next activity scheduled for the day. As we wait, a few of us start playing board games to pass the time, and I and a couple of other kids start playing chess. The board is sturdy cardboard and most of the pieces are there, except for a few black pawns that are missing and have been replaced with black checker pieces. I am not particularly good at the game but I enjoy it. As I set up the black pieces, my opponent, a White American boy the same age as I, sets up his white pieces. I know the kid; we get along some of the time, but honestly, whether he will be friendly on a given day is a coin toss. Ten minutes into the game, he gets frustrated because I have captured a few of his pieces, so he storms off and yells a phrase I have heard before and will hear again, "go back to where you came from!"

*

It is the autumn of 2001, school has started again, and I am going to the Boys & Girls Club for after-school programming since my parents work until 5 p.m. I get off the bus and make my way to the break room and line up with a bunch of the other kids to get something from a vending machine. A Black American boy who is a year or two younger and with whom I am vaguely acquainted, walks up and poses a question, "Can I borrow a dollar? I can pay you back in grapes."

*

It is the autumn of 2002 and I am living in Reidsville, North Carolina, and attending the county's high school. It is early morning, before classes have started, and I am waiting in the common area, sitting on the floor playing the card game Magic: The Gathering with two acquaintances. On the opposite side of the large room that serves as a kind of lobby between the different sections of the school, a group of Latinx students have started congregating and chatting as they wait for the morning bell. Off to my right there is another group of White American students gathering and talking, a collection of the self-styled rednecks who are identifiable by their common my-daddy-bought-it-for-me uniforms: a trucker hat with a fishhook attached to the brim, Carhartt coat, jeans, and work boots that have never actually been worked in. They are within earshot, and I hear one say clearly as they look over at the Latinx kids, "There sure are a lot of sandni**ers here."

About a month later, one of the rednecks decides to inquire about my racial identity. He is about a year older than I, a few inches shorter than I am, and is heavyset, appearing to be half-again my size. He marches up to me and, with my back against the wall, he demands to know if I am Mexican, something that he has apparently heard from someone else. I affirm that I am, and he proceeds to accuse me of being mixed because "full-blooded Mexicans can't speak English." Of course, the reality is that my dad is "full-blooded Mexican" and a native Spanish speaker who learned English through conversation and by watching American soap operas. Appropriately enough, he possessed a better grasp of English than this kid confronting me. The interrogation ends when the morning bell rings, and as the procession of students going to class leaves the common area empty, I am left standing there wondering what all this means for me as a 14-year-old in a new town, a new school, and with no real friends to speak of.

*

It is the spring of 2006 on a Saturday morning at 1:30 a.m., and I am passing through the edge of my hometown's limits into the countryside on my way home. I am going 40 mph in a 45 mph zone since I am tired and there are deer out, bounding across the road between sections of woodland. In my rearview mirror I see the same headlights that have been following me for almost ten minutes, but I do not think much of it until I see the blue flashing lights and hear the officer's siren. I pull my 1998 burgundy Ford Taurus over to the right side of the road and wait with my hands on the wheel, my heart pounding in my ears. This has never happened to me before, and I remind myself that I have not done anything wrong. The officer, an older White American man, walks up to my window as I roll it down. He asks me why I am driving slowly, and I respond that it is because it is late, I am tired, and I am concerned about deer. He asks where I have been and where I am going. I tell him I have been at a friend's house and

I am going home. He asks if I have been drinking, and I respond with a deferential "no, sir." He asks to see my license and registration, and I slowly retrieve my license from my wallet in my back pocket and the registration from the glove compartment. He takes them and walks back to his patrol car, and after a few minutes of my anxiously awaiting my fate, three cop cars pass by in quick succession. In that moment it occurs to me that he may have been expecting trouble before he spoke to me, but thankfully did not deem me a threat and so dismissed the backup. The officer eventually returns and lets me go without a citation or even a warning, just a few words about driving safely. In the moment I am thankful to drive away without getting a ticket that I would have to explain to my parents. Later, however, I would come to understand that he was probably engaging in a common pastime for law enforcement in my town: running plates and looking for drunk Mexicans.

*

It is 2011, and the heat and humidity of late summer is oppressive. My dad and I are working on a client's home. The job is to tear down his back deck and then replace it with a larger structure. I am dressed in work clothes: a baseball cap, a loose T-shirt, baggy jeans that are torn, and old sneakers, all of which are covered in paint and primer stains from years of remodeling houses. Dad handles the interactions with the client, who is a local high school teacher, so I have no reason to speak to him until around noon when dad leaves to go pick up lunch and I take a break after I have finished my assigned tasks. The client comes outside to check the progress on the project, when I ask him, "Excuse me, could I get a glass of water? It is really hot out here." The client pauses for a moment and blinks before replying, "Of course, I'll be right back." He returns with a glass of water, and as I drink, he remarks, "I'm sorry for the awkwardness, I didn't think I'd be able to communicate with you." I suppose I did not look like someone who would be starting a graduate program just a few weeks later.

*

It is August of 2019, just a couple of weeks after a White American man attacked a Walmart in El Paso, Texas, to kill people of Mexican descent and thus, in his mind, thwart the invasion of Mexicans entering the country. His rampage left 23 people dead, with many more people injured. It is a reminder of something that my family sometimes forgets: this country has a long history of killing Mexicans. The trauma from this tragedy has reached us in North Carolina, and it lingers in the air. It is one of the reasons my mom picked a fight with a sheriff's deputy at the local hospital during a visit for my sister. My mom had taken my high school-age sister to the local Emergency Room for a dance-related injury when they overheard a deputy talking about Mexican men as sexual predators. The night she confronted the man, she also spoke to his direct supervisor, and the next morning she spoke to a member of the command staff who answered directly to the sheriff. She recounts all of this to me over the phone in the evening, with a tone of cold restraint as she struggles to keep her disgust under control.. She tells me about her conversation with the high-ranking official and relays how she pressed him about the offending officer's comments. In response, the official said, "Ma'am, it is the understanding of this department that in Mexico, it is culturally normal for men to sexually abuse little girls." My mother verbally and intellectually flayed the skin from his bones, and as proud as I am to hear about her pushing back against him, I also know that it does not change anything.

Mass media mechanisms for racialization

The news media occupies a unique space within the mass media ecosystem. Whereas other types of media such as television, film, and streaming typically deal with fiction and the social imagination in terms of what *could* be, the news attempts to deal with reality as it exists. What is more, given the longevity of news broadcasting as an industry and its role within the United States as an institution that has played an integral part in helping to shape social reality, it is difficult to overstate the influence of the news on society. As such, it has also been vitally instrumental in the process of racialization for countless people who have lived within the United States, regardless of their ethnic background, economic level, or citizenship status.

There are two mass media concepts that illustrate powerful mechanisms for how the news operates as a tool of racialization, agenda setting and framing. In brief, these theories are used to explain how news programs influence audience perceptions of reality in particular ways. Agenda-setting theory asserts that news organizations determine what stories are important and thus receive attention in the form of news coverage, which serves to elevate their visibility for mainstream audiences. This increased visibility results in the perception by the audience that the news story in question is of particular importance (Luo et al., 2019). In effect, the programming agenda of news organizations shapes the public's agenda of important issues/news stories. This aspect of the theory is the first level of agenda setting, often referred to as the transmission of issue salience (Luo et al., 2019). Since its initial creation, a second level and third level have been added. The second level is the transmission of attribute salience, which is to say that not only does news programming shape which stories the public considers to be important, but the programming also influences what qualities and elements of news stories are of particular importance (Luo et al., 2019). The third level of agenda setting considers the ways in which issue salience and attribute salience are bundled together and then disseminated to shape public interest (Luo et al., 2019). To understand what this looks like, consider the issue of immigration from Mexico into the United States. The first level of agenda setting would address the high visibility of these stories, perhaps within the context of a particular political season, such as the year of a presidential election. The second level of agenda setting would be concerned with the aspects of immigration that receive a high degree of coverage, such as the economic impact or concerns about criminal activity. The third level of agenda setting would consider how the first two levels operate in tandem to shape the public's interest in immigration and what aspects of the issue would be of particular concern.

The concept of framing dovetails with agenda-setting theory, especially the transmission of attribute salience. Whereas the theory of agenda setting argues that the media influences what news stories and social issues the public determines to be important, framing refers to how news stories are constructed by journalists and how they are interpreted by audiences. On the macrolevel, framing considers how communicators such as journalists and news anchors present information in a way that will resonate with audiences (Scheufele and Tewksbury, 2007). On the micro level of audience interpretation, framing engages with how individuals use conceptual frameworks for making sense of the world to construct meaning from those same news stories (Scheufele and Tewksbury, 2007).

So, if agenda-setting theory says that the news tells us *what* to think about, then the concept of framing argues that the news also influences *how* to think about the issues covered in the news stories. The degree to which the ideologies advanced by news organizations are internalized by audiences is dependent on a variety of factors, such as frequency of media consumption, resonance with preexisting points of reference, and the volume of media that is consumed. However, what is undeniable is that news media, whether by design or consequence, enacts an ongoing project of racializing Latinx communities through agenda setting and framing. By elevating the visibility of news stories that tie Latinx identities to certain sociopolitical issues and framing them in a way that articulates *Latinidad* as an identity of non-White bodies, the news facilitates the process of racializing *Latinidad*. In the following section, I will address how this occurs through news coverage related to immigration, crime, and labor.

Dirty, dangerous, and displaced

Within US media, the prevailing depiction of Latinxs has historically been through the frames of immigration and criminality, often combining the two in the form of unauthorized immigration commonly referred to by the derogatory term "illegal immigration" (Dunaway et al., 2011). The use of the term "illegal" to describe those who immigrate from Latin America to the United States without authorization supports the cultural narrative that their presence in the United States is invasive; that is to say, not only is their entrance a violation of the law, but it is also a violation of the public will that does not consent to their presence. This Us versus Them dichotomy and the use of the term "illegals" as a pejorative is a component of the racialization of Latinxs as it positions us as incompatible with mainstream US society, with the implication that their personhood is irreconcilably different, not just legally but also racially, ethnically, and culturally. One way in which this race-based dichotomy has manifested is the existence of civilian border patrol militias and activist efforts, such as the Minuteman Project (MMP) of the early 2000s. Organizations like the MMP position themselves as the guardians of the United States and the people within it, with the clear understanding that they are interested in preserving their vision of a White-dominant society against hostile invasive forces (Heuman and Gonzalez, 2018). In the words of one member of the MMP, "The only way I'd be down here is with a bunch of other White guys with guns. Whites are the minority in these border towns, man. They've already been taken over. This is enemy territory" (Holthouse, 2005, para. 50).

While border patrol militias may appear to be extreme examples of this type of sentiment, they are by no means unique. Since the early 2000s, there has been a proliferation of groups that either overtly or implicitly utilize the same ethos of defending the United States from immigrant invaders. Groups like the Proud Boys, the Patriot Front, the Three Percenters, and the Oath Keepers all operate from a perspective of being the rightful inheritors of a Western (read: White) legacy that is in need of defense from corrupting swarms of foreign invaders. The negative depiction of Latinx immigrants within the news legitimizes their perspectives while making less overtly violent but still virulently dangerous ideological frames increasingly normative. My contention is not that mainstream news sources are radicalizing citizens to patrol the border or join what are in effect street gangs. Rather, my assertion is that the racialization of Latinxs that occurs through news media aids such groups by legitimizing their perspectives; and while these groups are the tip of the spear, the haft to which the tip is attached is the collective society of residents of the United States who passively participate in that racializing process by uncritically consuming the media and thus tacitly supporting the process.

This popular conceptualization of Latinxs as being foreign-born criminals who break the law to enter the country has implications beyond an audience's momentary consumption of a particular piece of media. The repeated use of stereotypes and patterns of depiction can create discursive formations within media called "controlling images" that inform the real-world decisions made by the audience. Controlling images "are the repetitive stereotypes that also possess the power to influence action and policies against people of color" (Deckard et al., 2020, p. 584). In effect, these controlling images create types of naturalized knowledge within the social imagination that informs the public's support for policies relative to the given demographic. In the case of Latinxs, these controlling images within the context of immigration heavily utilize two stereotypes in particular: bandidos and breeders.

Bandidos are Latinos, men whose most salient quality is the capacity for violence and illegal activity. More than that, the bandido is a man "whose very body represents a transgression of US laws and is thus outside the structured world of White Americans" (Deckard et al., 2020, p. 585). Whether they appear as Brown, faceless men trudging through the desert wilderness of the American Southwest, as bent-backed farm laborers picking crops, or as gang members stalking the inner city, their lack of legal status, whether overtly stated or strongly implied, positions them in the public's mind as a threat to the law and order of White American society. As such, they are racialized as perpetual non-White Others who are ostensibly incompatible with dominant society, the reliance of society on their unauthorized labor notwithstanding.

This connection between Latino masculine identity and criminality, and the attendant negative stereotypes, is deeply entrenched. Figueroa-Caballero and Mastro (2019) go so far as to assert that in terms of news coverage, it is difficult to find representations of undocumented immigrants that are not inextricably characterized by *Latinidad* or criminality, and often the depiction includes both. As such, Latinxs, and in particular Latinos, are accompanied by a perception of danger when they enter new environments, which leads local members of a given community to anticipate an increase in crime due to the presence of the Latinxs. This real-world manifestation of media-induced anxieties about the criminal threat posed by Latinx immigrants, referred to as the Brown

Threat by Cervantes, Alvord, and Menjívar (2018), illustrates the influence that media has on shaping the perceptions and behaviors of communities. But whereas controlling images of bandidos facilitate a sense of fear about the physical threat posed by Latinos, the controlling image of the breeder, which characterizes Latinas in the news media, facilitates a fear that Latinx people pose a threat by becoming a burden on society as well as by shifting demographics.

Breeders are Latinas whose reproductive capabilities are weaponized against the host country. This type of framing has its origin in news stories that portray Latin American women as being particularly adept at procreating, and who either bring their children to the United States or begin to have a high number of children once they enter the country. According to this controlling image, doing so drains resources and aids in the demographic shift within the United States (Deckard et al., 2020).

These binary controlling images of Latin American immigrants as threats to normative White American society are enough on their own to contaminate the dominant society's conceptualization of Latinx people as foreigners who pose an existential threat not just to the country but to its demographic future. Furthermore, once in the United States, Latinx communities are framed in the news as politically monolithic. As Gonzalez-Sobrino (2020) posits,

> in politics as well as in research, Latinos are constructed as a one-dimensional, monolithic ethnoracial category. In other words, Latinos are treated as one big, unchanging, and undifferentiated group of people who possess the same culture, the same interests, and the same political behaviors and attitudes. (p. 1027)

The supposition that Latinxs in the United States are a politically monolithic group strips away the complexities of the multitude of cultural perspectives, national identities, philosophies,
and behavioral norms and practices that characterize the many
subgroups which exist within the broader Latinx community.
We become homogenized into a voting bloc without regard
for even the most basic of realities of Latinx life: our respective
relationships with the policies of the United States as informed
by our own racialized experiences and the experiences of our
ancestors. Due to this mass-mediated construction of political
homogeneity, and combined with the controlling images of the
bandido and breeder, we are racially constructed as a demographic that is a threat not just to the communities we inhabit
and the social systems we are alleged to burden with children,
but also a threat to the political future of the country as a voting bloc. This is especially the case within the minds of conservative political commentators who frame us as a group loyal to
the Democratic Party, which is allegedly in favor of unrestricted
immigration; some even take it so far as to peddle in white nationalist conspiracy theories such as Tucker Carlson's allegation of the
"great replacement" (Bond, 2023). This conspiracy theory holds
that non-White immigrants are brought into the United States to
replace White American voters as a part of political strategy for
resisting conservative politics.

Even more dehumanizing than being characterized as a monolithic, invading force of criminals and a burden on society is the
reduction of Latinx people to pollution, to social contaminants.
The metaphor of pollution, detailed by Cisneros (2008) in the article "Contaminated Communities: The Metaphor of 'Immigrant as

Pollutant" in Media Representations of Immigration," simultaneously dehumanizes Latinx people while normalizing American identity as an identity based on racial and cultural "purity." White Americans are the heart of the country, and we are the poison that corrupts the body of society and threatens that heart. Consistent with the literature about Latinx people as immigrants, criminals, and a social burden, Cisneros (2008) identifies three ways in which the news uses the discourse of contamination and the metaphor of pollution to describe Latinx immigrants: social disruption and damage, the devastation of victims, and the need for containment. It is the last point, the need for containment, that is perhaps the most insidious as it serves as the justification for micro- and macrolevel enforcement of borders and the reification of racial stratification. Containment, as Cisneros (2008) explains, involves valorizing local efforts to regulate Latinx bodies through official regulators like police and sheriff departments as well as through civilian efforts such as the Minutemen border militia, while at the same time condemning federal forces for failing to contain the pollution. I would suggest that micro-level interactions between civilians wherein non-Latinx Americans harass and accost Latinx-perceived people is an extension of that desire for containment and another manifestation of the racialization process.

A warped window

The news media functions as a unique epistemological tool for learning about society, distinct from other forms of mass media. Whereas fictional television shows, films, and streaming media are underpinned by the conceit that they are at best approximations of reality, the news ostensibly presents itself as a window through which one perceives reality. This window, which may at first glance appear to be clear and expansive in scope, is still a human construct and thus subject to flaws and limitations. The clarity is colored by ideological bias, the glass itself is warped by editorial perspectives, and however broad the view appears, it is still bordered by a frame that limits what can be seen through the window. The comments, perspectives, and behaviors that I have experienced throughout my life, such as those detailed at the start of this chapter, were manifestations of what those people learned from the news media. Moments like those and countless others that have been experienced by those in Latinx communities are the interpersonal aspect of the project of racialization that is compounded by a vision of *Latinidad* which is foisted onto us directly by the news media.

The process of racialization involves two strategies that converge within every person: ascription and identification. Ascription refers to the ways in which an identity is placed onto an individual, and identification is the process of accepting in part or in totality that designation (Brown, Jones, and Becker, 2018). Mass-mediated depictions and discourse that frames Latinx bodies as dangerous, criminal, foreign, and a social burden ascribe oppressive conceptualizations of *Latinidad* both to Latinxs and in the minds of those who perceive Latinxs. Our consumption of this ideologically laden material means that we learn about ourselves through the language of racialization. This language is reinforced when we interact with those who have bought into this conceptualization of our communities and interact with us accordingly. Unlike popular fiction, this type of media presents itself as real, and so consumption without critique, whether by those of us in Latinx communities or outside of them, facilitates this racialization as being natural, normal, and thus true.

Learning about *Latinidad* through the ascribed qualities of being inclined toward criminality, of being a social burden, inherently foreign, and a thing to be contained to prevent a corrupting influence had an adverse effect on my self-concept, particularly in my youth. Through my uncritical consumption of the media as a kid, combined with my first-hand experiences with others, I began to regard my *Latinidad* as a stigmatized identity, a signifier of my status as a part of an underclass. As such, I saw myself as being incompatible with mainstream, respectable society. In keeping with the concept of *nepantla*, there was nowhere I could go to escape the converging boundaries of *Latinidad*, as conceptualized by the news, and the environments and people that were defined by American whiteness. The desire to be known beyond an ascribed, oppressively racialized identity, created the foundation of what would become internalized racism. This sense of discomfort, and at times self-hate, toward my *Latinidad* began to form in my early teens and festered until I confronted it in my mid-20s. Even now, at the age of 36, while I have largely shed my feeling of internalized racism, I still struggle with vestiges of identification with the version of *Latinidad* conceptualized by the news. The most salient manifestation of this internalized prejudice is a feeling of incompatibility with my role as a college educator. I believed that people like me do not belong in these environments for so long that it is still difficult to imagine myself as belonging in such a role, even though I have the letters PhD after my name. And so, my questions to you are: If you are

Latinx, to what extent have you identified with, and internalized, the controlling images and discursive formations of *Latinidad* used in the news that I have described here? And how have you, whether you are Latinx or not, participated in or rejected the process of racialized identity ascription?

4
Stereotypes and threats

It is around noon on a mid-December day in 2008, in the town of Juan Aldama, Zacatecas, Mexico. The sun is shining, the air is comfortably warm, and is made even more so by the occasional breeze. I have never wanted to die more in my life than at this moment. The day before, I made the mistake of trusting my dad and eating street food from a vendor. My mom had warned me that while he would be fine because he had grown up eating that kind of food, I would not be so lucky. I ignored her cautions and by the following morning, I began to form an intimate bond with my *abuela's* (grandmother's) guest bathroom as food poisoning ran roughshod through my body.

But today, my parents planned to go to Juan Aldama, a small town with a decent-sized shopping district that is about half an hour from my father's village, and they were not about to let something as trivial as my having food poisoning get in the way. Rather than allow me to continue communing with the toilet, they dragged me along, almost quite literally. That is how I ended up here, weak-kneed and damn near dehydrated as I struggle against the ordinarily-pleasant-but-at-the-moment-nauseating, overwhelming smell of leather in a well-established clothing store. The owner of the store, a heavy-set, older Mexican man wearing a nice hat and an even nicer mustache, greets us as my family enters. Between my lack of proficiency with Spanish and general state of physical discomfort, I am not able to understand much of what he is saying beyond pleasantries, but the message is clear enough: he is doing his dead-level best to make us feel welcome. He quickly notices the pallor of my face and excuses himself, and soon returns carrying a tray with four shot glasses filled with clear liquid. My mom balks at the idea of my drinking alcohol (I am 20 and so still not able legally to drink in the United States), but the proprietor explains that the *sotol*, a liquor made in the region, will help me feel better. Although skeptical, I graciously accept the drink and slowly sip it along with my parents and the owner.

Once we finish the drinks, the owner escorts my parents and two younger siblings around the store, showing them his best boots, hats, and assorted clothing. I sit in a chair and prepare myself for the worst, practicing in my mind how to say, "I need to use the bathroom" in Spanish for when the moment inevitably comes. Surprisingly, ten minutes pass and I actually begin to feel better. The nausea subsides, and while I am still a little weak, I no longer feel on the verge of emptying my stomach. Pleasantly surprised by my improved condition, I look for the owner to express my gratitude and find him showing cowboy hats to my parents. As I approach, the proprietor spots me and asks me to wait for just a moment; he departs and quickly returns with a particularly large, very well made, straw cowboy hat. Unlike the popular *cuatro en la cabina* style where the left and right sides are folded upright, this one has a wide brim that is relaxed and meant to provide shade. The brim style, along with the long, loose leather chin-strap that can be worn around the neck and allows the hat to hang on one's back or to keep it from blowing away in the wind, makes it clear that this hat is meant for use and not just for style.

The proprietor begins speaking to me, but between my fatigue and my already poor Spanish, I am not able to keep up so my mom translates. "He says it's a nice hat and that it should fit you well, and he wants you to try it," she says. Reluctantly, I accept the hat and put it on, and the proprietor has me stand in front of a mirror. I am a big guy, 6'0", 220lbs, and broad shouldered, with a head size to match my frame. Hats that are marked "one size fits most" are not always a sure thing for me. But the hat fits my head and my frame, as the brim is just a little broader than my shoulders.

The proprietor is all smiles and enthusiasm as he begins speaking again. "He wants to know how you like it," my mom says. As I look in the mirror, I begin to feel embarrassed. I feel like a punchline to a joke I had no part in writing. I am reminded of Speedy Gonzales and Slowpoke Rodriguez, Cinco de Mayo commercials that are so stereotypically racist they escape scrutiny by most folks, and that stupid chihuahua from the Taco Bell commercials in the late 90s–early 2000s that became the most salient "Mexican" cultural reference point for many Americans at the time. I am reminded of how every time I have seen *Mexicanidad* represented on tel-evision, it is for a joke at our expense, like our culture is reduci-ble to an image of a Brown man who wears a brightly colored *zarape*, a comically bushy mustache, and an oversized sombrero, who also speaks broken English with a funny accent. And that is if we are lucky enough to see rural Mexicans depicted on screen.

Most of the time, what we get is the ever present image of the Mexican-American *cholo* from East Los Angeles that litters the film and television landscape. Sometimes he is *the* bad guy in a given story, but more often than not, he is just *a* bad guy meant to add a sense of danger to the scene. I do not want to be those things. I do not want to fulfill the stereotypes other people have of me, and if that means not being Mexican in any kind of discernable way, then so be it. Better to deny that part of me than to be a joke for someone else.

"It's awfully big," I say nervously, thinking of how to get out of having to wear this thing. The middle-aged man's face shifts from jovial to serious, but still kind, as he walks in front of me, looks me in the eye, and begins speaking. "He says," my mom translates, "if you wear it like a joke, then people will laugh, but if you wear it seriously, others will take you seriously."

Mass-mediated narratives and ideological fragments

While the news media frames our understanding of reality, popular fiction as depicted in films and television shape our collective social imagination. The popular fiction of a time reflects the fears, anxieties, and ambitions of that moment. Fictional stories carry messages related to socioeconomic frustrations, cultural norms, and political concerns, among other aspects of society. On a macrolevel these narratives inform the media ecosystem into which we are born and influence everything from official public policy to social justice movements. On a micro level, these narratives become points of reference for those outside of a given community and for those inside of it. They inform the development of personal identity. They provide us with equipment for articulating our own experiences or with stereotypes that we struggle against. These pieces of popular culture work to bring us ever closer to a subject position within ideological structures that racialize us and position us within the sociocultural hierarchy of the United States.

In this chapter, I discuss popular media texts in the formats of film and television as vehicles for ideologies of oppression, racialization, and liberation, and how they inform the conceptualization of *Latinidad*, and by extension *Mexicanidad* and other iterations of Latinx identity, within the social imagination. In the previous chapter, I addressed how the news media functions to racialize Latinxs as various types of social burdens and threats; in this chapter I engage with the ways in which popular fiction narratives on the big and small screens facilitate the process of racialization as well. I begin with an explanation of the narrative paradigm and how narratives operate as ideological fragments and tools of learning and reasoning. I explore the narrative stereotypes that have characterized much of mass-mediated *Latinidad*, how those stereotypes construct a kind of racial logic conveyed through stories, and also how progress has been made in conceptualizing us in a more humane and multidimensional way. I conclude with a discussion of the real-world implications of these stereotypes, including how they facilitate negative in-group and intergroup perspectives as a result of stereotype threat.

All storytelling, whether fictional or not, involves the construction of a reality. It may be a reproduction of our own mundane world, one that is characterized by the fantastic, or somewhere in between the two ends of that spectrum, but whatever the nature of the world in that story, it is still informed by the lived experiences of one or more creators who exist in our world. As such, ideologies permeate these texts by informing their creation and the meaning that is constructed from them in the minds of audiences. Everything from characters to settings can be understood as symbolic representations of larger, abstract ideas that we find in our own reality. But what is of particular importance is the role of the narrative itself in conveying ideas that become presented as natural, as normal. When certain stories and methods of constructing characters become so mundane that they become cliché or stereotypical, then they have entered the realm of what I refer to as "of course" knowledge, as in, "of course the thugs in this crime procedural television show are Latino," or "of course the Latina is a maid that flirts with the homeowner." In order to understand how stories become "of course" points of reference, we first need to understand Walter Fisher's narrative paradigm and how it fits into mass media.

Fisher's (1984) narrative paradigm operates based on the perspective that when it comes to rational decision-making:

1.   Humans are storytellers.
2.   We make decisions based on what we consider to be good reasons.
3.   What constitutes good reasons is informed by various factors such as cultural context and language.
4.   Rationality is determined by narrative probability and narrative fidelity. In this context narrative probability refers to the internal coherence of the story, and narrative fidelity refers

to whether the story in question is consistent with other stories the person knows to be true.

5.   The world is composed of stories, and we must choose from among these stories to live in a way that we find desirable.

As Fisher (1984) puts it, "in short, good reasons are the stuff of stories, the means by which humans realize their nature as reasoning-valuing animals" (p. 8). A key element that is important for us in the context of this chapter is the idea of narrative rationality, which Fisher (1985) connects to the Aristotelian concept called phronesis, or practical wisdom. His assertion is that we use stories to reason and to develop approaches for dealing with practical, real-world circumstances. This idea of narrative rationality has been applied to the realm of mass media analysis by positioning media artifacts as vehicles for ideologies. This perspective, called narrative criticism,

> identifies arguments proposed as morals through storytelling, complete with characters, plot, and actions. A moral as used in narrative criticism, then, refers to the value-laden ideological argument a story proposes directly or indirectly (as well as intentionally or unintentionally) about how we ought to or ought not to believe or behave. (Sellnow, 2017, Ch. 3 para. 2)

Essentially, the idea of narrative rationality that was originally developed to explain how humans make sense of the world has been expanded to the realm of mass media by considering how narratives within our media ecosystem operate as vehicles for ideologies through the morals of the stories. The heroes, villains, settings, and narrative arcs become ideologically laden sites that suture stories in such a way that audiences can use them for reasoning and meaning-making. And so, every construction of reality through a narrative depicted on film or in television supports, subverts, or modifies an existing ideology.

Within the context of ideological structures, it is useful to think of pieces of media as fragments wherein each piece fits into a larger whole. Individually, each text is an easily digestible piece of content that the audience can consume and then form their own judgments. However, when viewed collectively, media fragments "can coalesce to form overarching narratives that dictate assumptions about a particular topic" (Atkinson and Calafell, 2009, p. 5). This means that rather than merely consuming the media, we become interpellated into the ideological structure; we become influenced by the repeated messages so that we perceive our world in a way that is consistent with the narratives we have consumed. I do not mean to suggest that there is a one-to-one relationship between consuming media and accepting the ideological morals that are proposed, but rather that as we consume messages repeatedly, we become susceptible to viewing the proposed narrative morals as reasonable and plausibly true. One example of this phenomenon is the relationship between the consumption of media and the perception of justice or danger within society. Scholars of cultivation theory, which contends that consumption of a given type of media informs perceptions of reality, affirm that the messages consumed by audiences are likely to influence their perceptions to align more closely with those messages depicted in television (Appel, 2008; Mastro, Behm-Morawitz, and Ortiz, 2007).

One of the overarching narratives that has coalesced into a normalized assumption is the racialization of *Latinidad* and how it has come to be represented on the screen. In his essay "Cultural Identity and Diaspora," Hall (1990) engages with the ways in which cinema, and by extension other forms of media representation, have an effect not just on how members of a racialized group are seen by others but also on how they see themselves. Hall (1990) writes,

> Every regime of representation is a regime of power formed, as Foucault reminds us, by the fatal couplet, "power/knowledge." But this kind of knowledge is internal, not external. It is one thing to position a subject or set of peoples as the Other of a dominant discourse. It is quite another thing to subject them to that "knowledge," not only as a matter of imposed will and domination, by the power of inner compulsion and subjective conformation to the norm. (pp. 225–226)

In the context of the United States, the regime of representation includes the racialization of Latinxs, which entails imagining what we are expected to look like, how we are expected to behave, and where we can be expected to be seen. In this vein of thinking, the scholar Lisa Flores (2016) asserts that there is an imminent need to examine the ways in which race is constructed rhetorically, and she proposes three ways to do so. The first is to *hear race* both as a matter of vernacular expression and language use as well as the socially situated voices of individuals and communities. The second approach she articulates is to *see race* in terms of how race is represented, both in terms of what is and is not visible. This includes the examination of racialized depictions of bodies, dominant discourse and vocabulary, and other ways that ideological constructs of race manifest socially, culturally, and politically. The third approach Flores proposes is the examination of the phenomenon of *bounding race*, which is how rhetoric is used to facilitate racial logics about nation, citizenship, and the matter of who belongs. Within the context of mass-mediated narratives developed in the United States, more often than not our voices have not been heard, our on-screen identities have been reduced to a collection of simplistic and insulting stereotypes, and we have often been relegated to being perpetual foreign Others. In the following section, I lay out the ways in which mass-mediated narratives have been used rhetorically to create normalized assumptions that have advanced the racialization of Latinx communities, as well as ways in which those oppressive discourses have been challenged.

Racialized stereotypes

In the United States, our mass media system, propped up by the film and television industries among others, functions in a way that supports the normalcy of whiteness and the stigmatization of non-White identities (Lopez, 2020). Non-White racial identities are often depicted in television and film in a way that marks them as non-normative Others, and *Latinidad* is no exception. When a non-White racialized identity is constructed as an Other on-screen, it is used to reinforce the centrality and superiority of whiteness (Oh and Kutufam, 2014), which in this case is tied directly to conceptualizations of what it means to be American. As mentioned earlier, media operates in an instructive manner and propagates cultural understandings about what constitutes normative society. Along with the assertion that mainstream media reinforces the centrality of whiteness and the marginalization of non-White identities, the end result is that the media endorses the messages that if you are White, you are the norm, a part of the status quo; and if you are not White, then the only real option for navigating society is assimilation into the mainstream (Stamps, 2019), if that is even an option. For many of us, full assimilation is not an option because of our immutable characteristics. For those who can assimilate, doing so may come at the expense of our aspects of ourselves that are tied to our core identities.

In the broader mainstream media ecosystem, a place has been carved out for Latinxs, which, as with other racial minority groups, is characterized by an abundance of stereotypes. These narrative shorthand caricatures take real-world, complex experiences, personalities, and identities that have been shaped by converging sociocultural, political, and historical forces, and boils them down into bite-sized fragments that are easily digestible for White American audiences, among others. Of course, that is when Latinxs are visible at all in mainstream media in the United States.

One proposed conceptual framework for considering the presence of Latinx stereotypes in mass media articulates four stages of development: 1.) invisibility/nonrecognition; 2.) visible and ridiculed; 3.) regulation and social control via depictions of involvement with the criminal justice system; and 4.) egalitarianism and complex representation (Rudolph, 2017). Moving forward, we will engage with the major stereotypes used to represent Latinx identities, many of which fall into the second and third stages of this framework. The goal of doing so is to render them visible so that we can challenge the structure that has treated them as normative and reflective of actual *Latinidad*. If we, as a society, are going to move firmly into the fourth stage of representation, then we must confront the dominant method of depicting Latinx identity (Navarro, 2017).

Historically, mass-mediated *Latinidad* has been characterized by unsavory qualities such as criminality, hypersexuality, low economic class status, and buffoonery (Tukachinsky, Mastro, and Yarchi, 2017). At the same time, portrayals of Latinxs have also followed a racial logic, because while the Latinx community includes people with skin colors from across the Black-White spectrum, there has always been a particular *look* to mass-mediated *Latinidad*: lighter-skinned but not White (in the conventional European sense) (Aldama and Gonzalez, 2019), such as Salma Hayek, Oscar Isaac, and America Ferrara. This racial logic of what it means to look Latinx along with the stigmatized character qualities have been combined into codified stereotypes that have been used for decades in modern film and television media, so that when Latinxs do appear on-screen, the depictions are often dehumanizing and racist.

In his foundational work *Latino Images in Film: Stereotypes, Subversion, & Resistance,* Charles Ramierez-Berg (2002) outlines six basic stereotypes: bandido, harlot, female clown, buffoon, Latin lover, and the dark lady. These six stereotypes form the basis for most mainstream depictions of Latinxs and thus contribute to how we are conceptualized in the social imagination.

El bandido

The bandido is among the oldest and most enduring of racialized stereotypes. It is rooted in one of Hollywood's most enduring film genres: the Western. These films are typically set in the American frontier during the period of imperial expansion across the territories that now constitute the western United States. The heroes are often rugged cowboys, icons of individualism and vigilante justice, who operate on the border of civilization and the untamed wilderness, and when the villains are not other cowboys or Native Americans, they are bandidos. In the early days of film, these characters were coded in a way that distinctly lacked any of the romantic elements associated with American cowboys. The bandido was framed as

> dirty and unkempt, usually displaying an unshaven face, missing teeth, and disheveled, oily hair. Scars and scowls complete the easily recognizable image. Behaviorally, he is vicious, cruel, treacherous, shifty, and dishonest; psychologically, he is irrational, overly emotional, and quick to resort to violence. His inability to speak English or his speaking English with a heavy Spanish accent is Hollywood's way of signaling his feeble intellect, a lack of brainpower that makes it impossible for him to plan or strategize successfully. (Ramirez-Berg, 2002, p. 68)

Additionally, the bandido is heavily associated with the infringement of US national sovereignty and does so by disrespecting the US border with Mexico, crossing over whenever he seeks to rob, kidnap, or generally assail good, peaceful White Americans (Rudolph, 2017). These early themes associated with the bandido of greed, violence, criminality, and foreignness have persisted as elements of the symbol throughout its various manifestations. Over time, the depiction of the bandido has changed from the antagonistic Mexican cowboy to the Latin American drug runner, or narco, and more recently the inner-city gang member (Ramirez-Berg, 2002).

While the details and aesthetics have changed with each iteration, the previously mentioned themes that have defined the character have remained the same. Notably, the inner-city gang member moves the frontier wilderness from the American southwestern border with Mexico to the heavily populated urban centers on the interior of the United States. Television shows like *Law and Order*, which has run for 20 plus seasons, use the Spanish language and the bodies of Latinx criminals to frame certain locations in population-dense cities as lawless spaces where the inhabitants are unAmerican and prone to violence (Rudolph, 2017), similar to the frontier of the American Southwest.

Aside from the parade of Latino men depicted as criminals in *Law and Order* and other crime procedural shows, the bandido can be seen in a variety of other contexts. The television series *Mayans M. C.* (2018), the spin-off of the popular series *Sons of Anarchy* (2008), centers around a motorcycle gang composed of Latinos who regularly engage in illicit activity. Whereas on crime procedural shows the Latinos are interchangeable to the point of being faceless, these characters serve as both the central protagonists and the antagonists to whom the audience develops emotional attachments. Even speculative fiction is not immune to the pervasive influence of reductive Latino stereotypes, as *Star Wars* makes use of the bandido figure as well. Oscar Isaac's character, Poe Dameron, is introduced in *Star Wars Episode VII: The Force Awakens* (2015), and over the course of the next two films, the character is depicted as a rugged, adventurous, and at times morally questionable, hero. However, in *Star Wars Episode IX: The*

Rise of Skywalker (2019), the audience learns that the character's backstory is that of having been a spice smuggler, the galactic version of a drug runner. Even in the vastness of space in a galaxy far, far away, these stereotypes prove to be inescapable. Such depictions contribute to the racialization of Brown Latinx men as foreign, dangerous, criminal, threatening, and inherently deficient in a way that supports the nativist racial hierarchy of the United States (Huber and Solorzano, 2015).

The harlot

The feminine counterpart to the bandido is the Latina harlot: a dangerous woman who is driven by her carnal passions, which are often directed toward a White man (Ramirez-Berg, 2002). In addition to their overt sensuality and seductive behavior, these types of women are characterized by "their heavy accent, exoticness, sexual aggressiveness, and fiery temper" (Figueroa-Caballero, Mastro, and Stamps, 2019, p. 273). These Latinas are often depicted as audibly and visually loud, with revealing clothing, vibrant makeup, and extravagant jewelry that matches the volume of their heavily Spanish-accented English (Casillas, Ferrada, and Hinojos, 2018). Often these characters are relegated to secondary or tertiary roles, background characters who have few if any lines and often exist relative to a man, that is, the wives and girlfriends of men who have more substantial speaking roles.

However, these characters are sometimes afforded more prominent roles in narratives. The character Chihuahua in John Ford's *My Darling Clementine* (1946), is an early example of this stereotype, and among her most salient characteristics is her sexually aggressive disposition, which results in her engaging in conflict with others (Ramirez-Berg, 2002). More recent, prominent examples of this stereotype include Maddy Perez (Alexa Demie) in *Euphoria* (2019) and Gloria Pritchett (Sofia Vergara) in *Modern Family* (2009). Both characters feature the hallmark attributes of the harlot: hypersexuality, aggression, the potential for violence, and romantic involvement with White American men. Yet these characters reflect both ends of the spectrum in terms of how this stereotype can be represented. For example, consider the role that their visual appearance plays in their respective series.

Euphoria is a drama that features high school students whose lives are defined by drugs, sex, and violence. Perez's narrative arcs include each of those aspects. The series began in 2019 on HBO, and is a clear example of television that is designed for mature audiences, as opposed to the more family-friendly series *Modern Family*. While the character of Gloria Pritchett does share some qualities with Perez, the character functions in a comedic capacity rather than in a darkly dramatic role. Both Perez and Pritchett wear clothing that reveals their bodies in a way that signifies an ever-present potential for immediately engaging in sexual activity, similar to that of a pin-up model (McGrath, 2007); however, this aspect of the characters functions differently in their respective contexts. For Perez, the revealing clothing that serves as her normal mode of dress visually distinguishes her from her non-Latinx peers and thematically dovetails with the on-screen depictions of Perez's sexual activity, which often have a sexually transgressive aspect. While Pritchett's clothing also distinguishes her from the non-Latinx characters on *Modern Family*, it is often used for comedic effect. For example, the first episode of the series introduced Gloria Pritchett, played by Sofia Vergara, who was 37 at the time, as the second wife of the family patriarch, Jay Pritchett, who was played by the 63-year-old Ed O'Neill. The age difference between the two serves as a long-running point of humor as other characters in the show confuse them for father and daughter rather than husband and wife. Gloria's form-fitting clothing serves to reinforce her youthful vibrancy, which stands in stark contrast to Jay's bland and geriatric aesthetic, thus adding to the comedic effect.

The female clown and male buffoon

It must be noted that the character of Gloria Pritchett not only possesses the qualities of the harlot stereotype, but she also functions as another stereotype: the female clown. Typically, the female clown is depicted as hypersexual and then has her sexuality negated so that the protagonist, usually a White American male, has a reason to reject her in favor of another character. Usually, this negation is done by framing the character as too silly, too comical, promiscuous, or engaged in some other socially stigmatized behavior such as crime (Ramirez-Berg, 2002). While Pritchett's sexuality is not negated, she is romantically involved with a White male protagonist, she is often framed in a comical way, and a vivid example of that is her vocal body. The term "vocal body" refers to "all aspects of a person's speech, such as perceived accent(s), intonation, speaking volume, and word choice" (Casillas, Ferrada, and Hinojos, 2018, p. 63). Gloria Pritchett's vocal body is characterized by English spoken with a heavy accent, dramatically apparent grammatical errors, and an intense volume (indicative of the stereotypical fiery temper), all of which are utilized to create moments of miscommunication for comedic purposes (Casillas, Ferrada, and Hinojos, 2018).

The masculine counterpart to the female clown is the male buffoon. This character often serves as comic relief, as the sidekick (Ramirez-Berg, 2002) who is unintelligent, inarticulate, and comically inept (Figueroa-Caballero, Mastro, and Stamps, 2019). A classic example of this type of character is the iconic Ricky Ricardo played by Desi Arnaz in the series *I Love Lucy*. While the character is portrayed as a loving husband and father, his mannerisms and attributes also frame the character as a cultural punchline for audiences. For example, the character speaks English with a particularly pronounced Spanish accent, a signifier of his Cuban origins, which often involves obvious mispronunciation, such as when he says, "Lucy, you got some 'splainin' to do," then launches into an explosive, emotional rant in Spanish (Ramirez-Berg, 2002). This pattern of Latinos serving as buffoons has persisted into the twenty-first century. The series *That 70s Show* ran from 1998 to 2006 and utilized the buffoon stereotype with Fez, played by Wilmer Valderrama, whose racialized otherness was a source of comedy (Aldama and Gonzalez, 2019). More recently, the stereotype has permeated the Marvel Cinematic Universe with Luis, as portrayed by Michael Peña. The character has appeared in *Ant-Man* (2015) and *Ant-Man and the Wasp* (2018) as a sidekick to Paul Rudd's titular Ant-Man/Scott Lang. Luis's buffoonery comes in the form of his comical social awkwardness and generally quirky behavior rather than using a specific aspect of *Latinidad* as a punchline such as a ridiculously heavy Spanish accent. Yet, while Luis's role as the buffoon is less rooted in a culturally specific aspect, his racialized identity as a phenotypically Brown Latino still marks him as an Other. This is particularly evident when he is depicted alongside his fellow ex-cons and business associates, who are also marked as racial or ethnic Others: Dave (T. I. Harris), who is a Black American, and Kurt (David Dastmalchian), who is Eastern European. To be clear, this is an improvement over previous iterations of the stereotype where the identity was the joke, but it still serves as an example of a Latino relegated to sidekick status and to serving as the comedic relief.

The Latin lover

Whereas the bandido stereotype emphasizes the aspect of danger and the buffoon is defined by comedy, the Latin lover's most salient quality is hypersexuality, particularly in the capacity of being the romantic pursuer. This innate attractiveness is combined with the element of danger in a way that frames the character through themes of "eroticism, exoticism, tenderness tinged with violence and danger, all adding up to the romantic promise that, sexually, things could very well get out of control" (Ramirez-Berg, 2002, p. 76). In the early years of film, actors such as Rudolph Valentino and Ricardo Montalbán embodied these qualities in the characters they played, characters who were framed as attractive in ways that White American leading men couldn't be (according to the logic of the films) (Ramirez-Berg, 2002). While this stereotype has persisted, its depiction has also evolved. In 2017, the Mexican Eugenio Derbez starred as Maximo in the comedy film *How to be a Latin Lover* (2017). Maximo, the Latin lover in question, has not aged well and struggles with navigating the realities of no longer being young and handsome after his much older and wealthier wife, whom he seduced years prior, replaces him with a much younger man. In order to return to a life of luxury, he attempts to seduce an older, rich widow, Celeste (Raquel Welch). His attempts at doing so create much of the humor in the film, such as dyeing his chest hair so that it is no longer gray, only for it to wash out while swimming in a pool. His desperate attempts to seduce women frame the character as shallow and self-centered. Such a depiction borrows from the buffoon stereotype and turns the character into a punchline for American audiences to laugh at, rather than with.

Whereas Derbez's character Maximo takes a comedic approach to the stereotype, the character Oberyn Martell, played by the Chilean actor Pedro Pascal in HBO's *Game of Thrones*, takes the stereotype in a decidedly different direction. Martell is a member of the royal family of Dorne, a country within the fictional series created by author George R. R. Martin. While the television series and the books that it is based on take place in a fantasy world, Martell embodies the Latin lover stereotype. The character comes from a region where the people are racialized as broadly non-White, as opposed to many of the main characters who are racialized as White with European features and aesthetics. This makes sense because the creator has stated that Moorish Spain, among other aspects of European history, influenced the creation of Dorne (Guxens, 2012). The character has an established reputation for being a prolific lover of women and men, as well as being an extraordinarily dangerous combatant. That the character was played by a Latin American actor emphasizes the point, particularly since Pascal's light-skinned appearance stood out in stark contrast to the pale complexions of the other major characters and thus reinforced his exotic otherness. Martell's indulgence in violence and desire to avenge the death of his sister, Elia Martell, ultimately proves to be his downfall as he is killed in ritual combat by his sister's murderer, Gregor "The Mountain" Clegane, when Clegane crushes Oberyn's head using his hands. Yet another example of Latinxs being doomed by their passion.

The dark lady

The dark lady stereotype puts a spin on the idea of Latinx stereotypes being defined by excessive qualities. Whereas others are characterized by highly visible signifiers such as violence and hypersexuality, the dark lady is defined by aloofness, reserve, and a sense of mystery. As Ramirez-Berg (2002) writes,

> The female Latin lover is virginal, inscrutable, aristocratic—and erotically appealing precisely because of these characteristics. Her cool distance is what makes her fascinating to Anglo males. In comparison with the Anglo woman, she is circumspect and aloof where her Anglo sister is direct and forthright, reserved where the Anglo female is boisterous, opaque where the Anglo woman is transparent. (p. 76)

Ramirez-Berg (2002) continues by providing examples of the dark lady from the twentieth century such as characters played by the Mexican actress Dolores del Río in films from the 1930s and 1940s, as well as Cuban actress María Conchita Alonso in the 1980s. This stereotype has persisted into the twenty-first century with characters such as Wednesday Addams (Jenna Ortega) in the Netflix series *Wednesday* (2022), and Rosa Diaz (Stephanie Beatriz) in *Brooklyn Nine-Nine* (2013). Wednesday is racialized as Latina through the portrayal of the character by the Puerto

Rican/Mexican-American actress Jenna Ortega as well as by extension of the character's father, Gomez Addams, being played by the Puerto Rican actor Luis Guzmán. And while there is little else about the character to suggest that the character is Latina, she still fits firmly into the dark lady stereotype. She is from an ostensibly aristocratic family, her cold and hostile demeanor convey a sense of aloofness and make her inscrutable, and she is sexually reserved. In fact, in the series the character experiences her first kiss, which suggests that this was her first sexual contact. The only significant deviation from that stereotype is that she is a teenage girl, as opposed to the adult women who have typically represented the stereotype, although even that aspect of the character could change in future adaptations.

In the series *Brooklyn Nine-Nine*, the character Rosa Diaz is portrayed by the Argentine American actress Stephanie Beatriz. Rosa's character construction leans heavily on the dark lady stereotype: her consistent level of hostility and aggression makes her appear to be often emotionally opaque and distant; the character attempts to keep her personal life and romantic relationships private from others, thus creating a sense of mystery about the character; and while she is not a member of the aristocracy, she is a police officer, which is an occupation that has historically and contemporarily enjoyed an elevated social status. Even though the character is not virginal, she is romantically inaccessible to all of the other characters with whom she works, which creates a sense of sexual reservedness about the character.

Wearing the hat

All of these stereotypes are unified by the concepts of extravagance and exaggeration, in clear distinction from the reasonable (read: White) norms. (Aldama and Gonzalez, 2019). Whether that is hyperviolence (bandido), comedy (male buffoon and female clown), sexuality (Latin lover and the harlot), or mystery (dark lady), Latinxs are often constructed with exaggerated qualities, when we are seen at all. Returning to the story that I shared at the start of this chapter, at that time I considered the hat (and indeed any other external markers of *Latinidad*) a signifier of that exaggerated identity. I had consumed two decades worth of media that framed Latinx people as either undesirably violent and unknowable, or as absurd and comedic, and so the identity markers for *Latinidad* were associated with stigmas. They indicated that a person was either something to be rejected or accepted so long as they served as a punchline for White Americans to laugh at. And because I grew up in environments primarily occupied by White Americans, I had learned to laugh at those characters as well. I had decided, whether intentionally or not, that I needed to align myself with whiteness in order to fit in, and that meant rejecting any signifier of a racialized Other. Of course, this ideological alignment didn't result in my being accepted as White, at least not consistently. I can pass as White conditionally, depending on the environment and the perspectives of those that I'm around and how they make sense of my appearance, but typically speaking, I'm more often than not identified as a person of color. Buying and wearing a cowboy hat, or any other piece of clothing with a Mexican western aesthetic, would reinforce that perception. What this process of assimilation did consistently result in was a sense of internalized racism, a feeling that I should be ashamed of that which kept me from whiteness. I rejected my *Latinidad* and began to regard it as external to me, as something to be avoided, as something undesirable. To revisit the concept of *nepantla*, the in-between space, I stood on a biracial, bi-ethnic boundary and desperately tried to pick the side that aligned with whiteness, but the result was that I found myself with one foot in two different worlds and I resented the Mexican side of that border.

A few years later, I would begin to grapple with my sense of internalized racism, and in the years since buying that hat, I have shifted toward embracing my *Norteño* Mexican identity. It certainly helps that media representations of Latinxs, while still troubling, have made significant strides forward. Series like *The George Lopez Show* (2002) proved to mainstream American audiences that it is possible for Latinxs to be funny in a normative work/home sitcom format in English language programming where Latinxs are the center of the narrative and not just sidekicks inserted for comedic relief (Avilés-Santiago, 2019). The series *Ugly Betty* (2006), *Jane the Virgin* (2014), *Shades of Blue* (2016), and *Superstore* (2015) all feature Latinas in leading roles (Avilés-Santiago, 2019). And while these series are not without their critiques, such as America Ferrera's titular character, Betty, gradually leaving behind her *Latinidad* as she becomes increasingly successful at her job (Aldama and Gonzalez, 2019), these shows still paved the way for better quality Latina representation on screen.

While live-action films and television series have made strides, animated children's media may be where progress has been the most evident. We are a long way from Speedy Gonzales (Freleng, 1955), and Baba Looey (Barbera and Hanna, 1959). With characters like Rosita on *Sesame Street* (Squires, Stone, Simon, and May, 1991) and animated series like *Dora the Explorer* (Weiner, Gifford, and Valdes, 2000), *Maya & Miguel* (Forte, Dorta, and Richman, 2004), *Go, Diego! Go!* (Valdes and Gifford, 2005), and *Handy Manny* (Fellow, Bollen, and Sadler, 2006), Latinx representation has come a long way toward being more dimensional and humanizing (Avilés-Santiago, 2019). Additionally, films like *Coco* (Unkrich and Molina, 2017) and *Encanto* (Bush, Howard, and Smith, 2021) have continued to carry this forward momentum by further dimensionalizing *Latinidad* through centering characters and stories that allow for engaging with various aspects of different Latinx communities.

It is exceedingly important that this progress continue. Research on the cognitive effects of media on audiences indicates that stereotypes in mass media influence the way that non-Latinxs perceive Latinxs (Mastro, Behm-Morawitz, and Ortiz, 2007; Tukachinsky, Mastro, and Yarchi, 2017; Erba, 2018). Unfortunately, there is also evidence that negative, stereotypical representations of Latinx people can also facilitate negative attitudes toward one's own Latinx group (Tukachinsky, Mastro, and Yarchi, 2017). These depictions of Latinx identities graft racist perspectives onto the bodies of the people of color who portray these characters. In doing so, they act as visual microaggressions that remind audiences, White and non-White, that to be Latinx is to look a particular way, to behave in a particular manner, and thus by necessity they remain on the margins of society (Huber and Solorzano, 2015). These visual microaggressions contribute to the concerns that Latinx people may have about being perceived in a way that confirms one or more stereotypes about Latinx identity, a phenomenon known as stereotype threat (Erba, 2018). These reminders prompt Latinxs who seek to navigate mainstream society, to make choices about how they behave since behavior is easier to alter than one's skin tone. As Erba (2018) posits, "In other words, people may consciously change their behavior to avoid acting in a way that may be perceived as confirming a stereotype about their group" (p. 86).

This historic and ongoing construction of *Latinidad* within mass media through various stereotypes sutured onto Brown bodies creates, as Hall (1990) articulated, "a regime of representation." The internalization of these perspectives moves Latinxs into subject positions wherein they are incentivized to assimilate, to conform to this regime at the expense of positive self-concept, community, and cultural capital. While I maintain an optimistic disposition because of the progress that has been made, such efforts are still in a relatively nascent stage and will take time to mature.

5
Articulated Latinx heroism

It is the summer of 1998, I am ten years old, and I am standing in a home that is more museum than place of residence. My grandparents' home in Manassas, Virginia, is decorated with valuable artifacts in almost every room. Antique crackle glass, cookie jars from the early twentieth century, paintings, paperweights, vintage furniture, porcelain sculptures, and so on; and there is so much that walking through a hallway is an exercise in anxious self-awareness for any kid with enough sense to fear the consequences of bumping into something. I am standing in the living room, where no one really does any living since that is the room with the highest concentration of antiques, and my grandfather is holding a stack of comics. My maternal grandfather, whom I have always known as my "Boppa," is an active 50-year-old who works for the federal government in the Fish and Wildlife Service. He moved to Manassas several years prior with my Nana when he accepted a promotion from being a fish hatchery manager to overseeing multiple hatcheries in a specific region of the Southeastern United States. At this point in his personal timeline, he is on the cusp of requesting a transfer to a fish hatchery in Georgia where he can finish out his career far away from the bureaucracy and politics of Washington, DC, that are wearing him thin. The veteran nerd who cut his teeth on Edgar R. Burroughs, Robert A. Heinlein, and J. R. R. Tolkien hands me the comic books.

"Here you go," he says, "I think you'll find these interesting." I begin to flip through the collection, scanning the covers. Superman and Lobo exchange devastating blows on the cover of *Superman: The Man of Steel* #30. The Native American warrior Turok draws his bow and arrow at the reader as he scowls on the cover of *Turok: Dinosaur Hunter* #34. A man drops his rifle as a xenomorph face-hugger delivers its lethal embrace on the front of *Aliens Versus Predator War* #2. I keep flipping through the stack. A veiny, muscle-bound figure with a monstrous, humanoid face and a bloody, bladed gauntlet fused to his flesh grins sadistically on the cover of *Grendel: War Child* #1; at the bottom, beside the Dark Horse Comics logo, is the warning "Not For Children." So far, not much has really caught my attention until I see the cover of *Spider-Man 2099* #7. I know who Spider-Man is. A few of his comics are in this stack, but this is not the Spider-Man I know. This one has a different suit with red markings that look a little bit like *papel picado* in the shape of a skull, and he has spikes on his forearms. At the bottom of the cover are the words "Vulture 2099," but the Vulture I know looks nothing like this metal-winged, taloned villain. I glance through the rest of the stack and confirm that there are other issues of *Spider-Man 2099*. This is where I will start.

When my grandfather was old enough, he dropped out of high school and joined the navy. For much of his youth, he was a man on the run. He ran away from home and jumped on a ship. On the ship he ran away from good judgment and spent more than his fair share of days in the brig. He ran from the navy and

went home, where he ran from responsibilities until my grandmother demanded that he get his act together. And even then,
he decided to be a fish hatchery manager, which allowed him to
run away from large population centers … for a time anyway. But
even when he settled down, had a family, and fulfilled his responsibilities, he still ran away. It is just that he ran away to escapism.
He ran to alien worlds and high adventure. When he handed me
that stack of comic books, which are still in my collection more
than 20 years later, I am sure he thought he was giving me a
chance to run away for a little while. And to a certain extent, he
was. But more importantly he was giving me language.

I had lived in Manassas for about two years at that point. I was the
only Latino in my class, maybe in the entire fourth grade as far as
I knew. Manassas was the first time I did not have a community of
Latinx people around me. It was the first time I encountered clas-
sism as I was bullied for wearing thrift store and Walmart clothes.
I was different from the firmly middle-to-upper-middle-class
White American kids that I went to school with, whose parents
worked in places like DC.

The characters in those comics, like Bruce Banner or Peter Parker,
were different as well. Banner was cursed with the Hulk persona,
and Parker just could not catch a break from things going ter-
ribly wrong. But Miguel O'Hara, the Spider-Man of *Spider-Man
2099*, was Latino like me. And he was often the only Latino in
his books, like I was the only Latino in my class. These comics
sparked my love of superhero narratives, and because so many
of them centered around aspects of difference and being an outsider, they gave me a language for being able to articulate my
sense of otherness. And at the same time, the *nepantla* I knew,

the conceptual terrain that my identity occupied, was shifting yet again as it came to include the border between "Other" and "Hero." In the figure of Miguel O'Hara, the gap between the worlds of "ostracized" and "heroic" disappeared and the two shared a border; there was friction where they made contact, but they were connected all the same. A few years later, the reruns of *X-Men: The Animated Series* and then the brand-new show, *X-Men: Evolution*, would provide me with even more language for being able to identify and grapple with how I felt so different in White-dominant spaces, through their stories about mutants struggling against bigotry and oppression. Superhero stories are often dismissed as superficial children's entertainment, but the truth is, and I say this as a fan and as a scholar, they are valuable art forms that provide us with the tools to see ourselves and our world differently and more clearly.

Comics as a medium for social commentary

Receiving that stack of comic books from my grandfather was a critical moment in my life that cemented my interest in superheroes and, unknown to either of us at the time, their use as vehicles for social commentary. Speculative fiction, an umbrella term that includes science fiction, magical realism, high fantasy, and other genres characterized by departures from reality, is no stranger to sociocultural and political commentary. The genre of superhero narratives fits into this broad category and has continued that pattern productively since its creation in the 1930s–1940s with characters like Superman, Batman, Wonder Woman, and Captain America. It is important to note that moving forward, when I refer to superhero narratives specifically, I am including a variety of formats such as comic books, graphic novels, traditional books, animated and live action films and television series, and any other mediums of storytelling. Superheroes and comic books are often conflated, but it would be erroneous to use the terms interchangeably as comic books include a variety of fiction and nonfiction genres. While superhero narratives are perhaps the most visible genre associated with comic books, they are by no means representative of even the majority of the medium. In this chapter I discuss how stories about Latinx superheroes have become tools for engaging social commentary, specifically in terms of their roles as ideologically formed icons of identity. I examine the ways in which Latinx heroes have been constructed in prosocial and antisocial ways, interrogating the tropes, cliches, stereotypes, and innovations that have served as the building blocks for creating these characters. In order to thoroughly explore how Latinx superheroes operate as ideological formations, I first discuss how superhero narratives have often served as tools for engaging with social commentary. I then discuss the concept of articulation and how mass media discourse creates seamless connections between ideas that are not inherently tied to one another. Last, I explore how Latinx superheroes have been constructed, the articulations that make up their qualities, and how they operate as value-laden symbols in our collective social imagination.

It is tempting to dismiss superheroes as long-underwear adventurers who are little more than children's playthings, but in truth they are artifacts that reflect the complex social imaginaries of their eras. As comic book scholars Chambliss, Donaldson, and

Svitavsky (2013) so clearly articulate, "simultaneously affecting and being affected by society, the superhero genre highlights the struggle between American ideals and shifting social, political, and economic realities" (p. 1). Superheroes are symbols of their cultural moment, speaking to the hopes, fears, aspirations, and anxieties of their creators and finding resonance among audiences. In this way, superhero narratives function as cultural myths wherein the heroes, villains, victims, settings, and other details are drawn from real-world cultural elements and so engage with dominant norms, values, and beliefs, often, although not exclusively, in a conservative way (Chambliss, Donaldson, and Svitavsky, 2013). Conservative in this context refers to those ideologies that maintain the status quo, and not necessarily conservative in the political sense, although in the case of comics the two meanings have often been intimately linked. The basic premise of superhero narratives is that they "save the day" from villains and thus return society to its normative method of operation, validating established systems and hierarchies that enable it to function. As such, superheroes often act in a way that reflects the dominant society's fundamental beliefs about how morality, justice, and heroism are conceptualized; and attendant to that are notions about how people ought to be in terms of the expression of their various identities (Millán, 2016).

Early superhero narratives in comics were considered to be children's entertainment, which was a considerable factor in their utility as tools of ideological persuasion. Since comic books were easy to understand, rhetorically direct, popular, and typically involved characters displaying heightened emotion combined with intense action, they were particularly well suited to propagating dominant ideologies (Hirsch, 2014). While they may not have appeared to be political to readers in the early years of the 1930s–1950s, often referred to as the Golden Age of comics, they were absolutely saturated with political commentary. As Skidmore and Skidmore (1983) assert,

> Certainly most children of the Golden Age had no notion that their comics were propaganda. The critics centered their attacks upon portrayals of violence and crime, never upon ideology, except insofar as an occasional psychiatrist might complain that the worship of superheroes might induce Fascism. Nevertheless, a substantial portion of comic books have in fact always been intensely political. In the Golden Age, they were chauvinistic, they assumed that in every situation right and wrong were clearly distinct, and they forcefully set forth the United States as the embodiment of all that is right. Moreover, they frequently were overtly racist, sometimes even to the point of including stereotyped "Sambo" characters in attempts at comic relief. The prevailing attitude was well captured during the Second World War by the Golden Age Captain America, who often expressed his opinion that with regard to "Japs," the only task was to "Keep 'em dying! (Skidmore and Skidmore, 1983, p. 84)

Since the precedent was set in the Golden Age, superhero narratives have continued to operate as vehicles for ideological transmission, but unlike in the Golden Age, subsequent eras of comics and superhero narratives have often been ideologically complex and diverse. In recent decades, superhero narratives have been used to confront social ills such as racial discrimination (Nama, 2011), sexism (D'Amore, 2008), oppressive political ideologies

(Gledhill, 2016), and colonialism (Cruz, 2021). However, while the writers, artists, and editors have become increasingly diverse, as have the stories, a consistent theme in the narratives is that the implicit norm has been and continues to be White masculinity (Guynes and Lund, 2020). As Oyola (2020) posits, the ideological concept of whiteness is at the core of the genre of superhero narratives and attempts at disrupting that centrality often results in the narratives re-centering whiteness as the norm. Creative choices like race-bending characters (adapting a character to another story and changing their race from the original identity) and passing on legacy monikers to new characters of color (i.e., Sam Wilson, an African American who became Captain America; Amadeus Cho, a Korean American who adopted the moniker of The Hulk) still rely on the original White character as the referent and the new character exists in their shadow. Of course, there are examples of new heroes of color that exist on their own without relying on a White hero's name recognition, but more often than not it is only a matter of time before such characters are canceled due to poor sales and then fade into the background superhero milieu only to reappear occasionally as part of a team (Guynes and Lund, 2020).

However, it must be understood that such disruptions are evidence of the potential for change. In their edited anthology, *Graphic Borders: Latino Comic Books Past, Present, and Future,* Aldama and Gonzalez (2016) assert that the medium of comic books, and the attendant superhero narratives, has proven to be a platform for subverting denigrating stereotypes. While stories about racial minorities face an uphill struggle to gain the traction and popularity necessary to establish those characters as staples of the entertainment industry, the relatively low production cost of comic books (as compared to television series and films) means that it becomes less costly to experiment with innovative stories and new heroes. And as in the case of characters like Miles Morales/Spider-Man, America Chavez, Robbie Reyes/Ghost Rider, and Maya Lopez/Echo, this experimentation can lead to mainstream prominence and success. As with other popular culture symbols, these characters and their stories are cultural artifacts that operate as sites of struggle; it is ambiguity that allows for multiple competing, and at times conflicting, interpretations (Bucciferro, 2016). Additionally, they bear a burden not typically foisted upon their White counterparts; as the prominent African-American comic book creator Dwayne McDuffie explains, "my problem […] and I'll speak as a writer now […] with writing a black character in either the Marvel or DC universe is that he is not a man. He is a symbol" (Nama, 2011, p. 1).

Latinx superheroes, like other racialized characters in the genre, exist on a conceptual borderland between the world of an entertainment industry almost completely defined by whiteness, and the audience that they are attempting to represent, who have been shaped and oppressed by the circulation of whiteness. As McDuffie asserts, characters of color are not afforded the dimensionality of being seen as singular individuals; they are symbols that represent an entire group of people to those same people and to those outside of that group. I agree with this assertion, and in this chapter I position Latinx superheroes as mass-mediated symbols that are articulated in ways which embody the struggle of being produced by systems of whiteness while trying to speak to Latinx identities. In the following section, I discuss the concept of articulation as developed by Hall, and afterward I explore how sociocultural and political elements have formed the articulations that make up these symbols.

Stuart Hall and articulation

The concept of articulation can be understood as an idea that operates in three aspects: hegemony, conditions, and connections. Hegemony explains how members of a dominant class or actors with sufficient influence and access to systems of cultural knowledge maintain the interests of subaltern social groups such that they consent to a subordinated status, thus upholding the system that keeps them in place (Slack, 1996). Hegemony can be understood as the glue that maintains society, and by accepting positions of subordination we consent to the cultural leadership of the dominant class. Shifts, changes, and developments in social structures, such as the American civil rights movement of the 1960s and 1970s, alter society's hegemonic formation by disrupting the social order and advancing certain perspectives about what constitutes the interests of marginalized groups. As a result, new dynamics of subordination and domination are negotiated, thus resulting in a new hegemony. This leads to the second aspect of articulation: conditions. Just as societal conditions shape hegemony, hegemony in turn cultivates historical conditions that manifest as political movements, cultural norms, popular culture, and so on. These conditions prompt people to adopt ideologies that help them to make sense of the society as it exists, as they fear it could become, and as they believe it should be.

Conditions create the circumstances in which connections, the third aspect of articulation, occur. In this context, connections are the linkages made between ideas that are not inherently bound together but become merged through discourse (Hall, 2019). As Hall explains,

> But we also speak of an "articulated" lorry [truck]: a lorry where the front [cab] and back [trailer] can, but need not necessarily, be connected to one another. The two parts are connected to each other, but through a specific linkage, that can be broken. An articulation is thus the form of the connection that can make a unity of two different elements, under certain conditions. It is a linkage which is not necessary, determined, absolute, and essential for all time. (Hall, 2019, pp. 234–235)

Like trucks, popular culture texts are human works of artifice. Just as a truck is an assemblage of parts, popular culture artifacts are assemblages of symbols that are used to create meaning. Whereas a truck can be used to haul lumber, artifacts are used to transport ideologies.

In the case of superhero narratives, the articulations that form the characters include elements such as their cultural backgrounds, immutable identities, civilian lives, superhero monikers, body type, costumes, the villains they fight, their narrative arcs, and so forth. Each subsequent iteration of a given character is a new assemblage of symbols, including those that have already been associated with the character, some that are being utilized for the first time, and others that were associated with the character but have been rejected, thus sharpening the contrast between a current iteration and its predecessor(s). To locate superhero construction within the context of the three aspects of articulation, a specific character construction is formed by the connection of elements that are not inherently related but become articulated within the construction. These articulations are the result of the production studios, executives, and creatives that are attempting to appeal to audiences within a particular historical moment—a conjuncture defined by a variety of social, cultural, political, and economic factors (such as international conflicts, economic depression, civil rights efforts, etc.). Once created, these characters exist relative to the real-world ideologies that shape society and inform audience perceptions and thus endorse, modify, subvert, or resist those ideologies. In this way, these characters exist relative to the cultural hegemony of society, reinforcing problematic ideologies or challenging them to facilitate more humanizing conceptualizations of identity groups. This ability to challenge existing problematic ideologies in favor of counter-hegemonic conceptualizations of identity is possible because of the malleability of articulations. As Clarke (2015) posits,

> No articulation—whether the combination of social instances in a social formation or a discursive alignment of meanings and politics—came with a "lifetime guarantee." Rather their internal organisation (involving potential disjunctures, contradictions, antagonisms and tensions) and their external conditions of existence created the possibility of "disarticulation and rearticulation." (p. 277)

The impermanence of articulations and the possibility of their deconstruction and rearticulation open up opportunities for dominant hegemonies to be disrupted. Thus, new iterations of superheroes become new opportunities to rearticulate what it means to be a member of a particular identity group. This malleability conceptually dovetails with the symbolic significance of the "x" in "Latinx," which can be understood as a visual signifier of the unknown, unbound, and unfinished aspect of *Latinidad*. In this context of storytelling and narrative constructions of identity, the letter "x" invites us to speculate in imaginative, surreal, and fantastic ways where conceptualizing *Latinidad* is not constrained by the rigidity of nonfiction (Hudson, 2019).

In the following section, I discuss the ways in which Latinx characters have been constructed within the speculative fiction genre of superhero narratives. In the process I examine the various concepts that have been articulated within these symbols of *Latinidad* and address the positive and negative implications of these ideological manifestations.

Superheroes and *Latinidad*

Since the focus of this chapter is the examination of Latinx superheroes as articulated representations, I will focus on the "Big 2" publishers: DC Comics and Marvel Comics. To be clear, these are not the only two comic book publishers to tell stories about Latinxs. Less well known, but still vitally important, publishers like Fantagraphics and Image Comics have been hiring Latinx creators and selling comics featuring Latinx characters for years. Furthermore, self-publishing has become increasingly viable as characters like El Peso Hero, by Hector Rodriguez, and La Borinqueña, by Edgardo Miranda-Rodriguez, have demonstrated. While these stories and their creators play an important role in constructing the social fabric of alternative storytelling, they do not come close to exerting the mainstream influence of the Big 2 publishers. Even though film and television adaptations of less popular superheroes from smaller publishers abound, Marvel and DC are in a league of their own in terms of the reach and popularity of their intellectual property. And yet, for all of their resources and creativity, these publishers continue to place whiteness at the center of their imaginations, often relegating Latinxs to the margins of their narratives (Montes, 2016).

It is also important to acknowledge that as few Latinx superheroes as there are, Latinx supervillains are even less prevalent. Rarely do Latinx villains created by Marvel and DC achieve the level of visibility attained by their heroes. It is far more common for villainous Latinxs to appear as street-level criminals or villain-of-the-week antagonists who appear periodically, but without significant depth or dimensionality; they are frequently the types of repackaged tropes and stereotypes that have been used in television and film (as discussed in chapter 4 of this book).

One notable exception to this rule is DC's Bane, the first villain to "break the bat" in the classic story *Batman: Knightfall*. The character has been adapted to mediums other than comic books several times, the highest-profile adaptation being the version of the character portrayed by Tom Hardy in the 2012 film *The Dark Knight Rises*. Unfortunately, the Christopher Nolan version of the character was dramatically altered. Instead of being depicted as an intellectual genius and leader in his own right with a backstory rooted in Latin America, the character was transformed into a henchman for the League of Shadows and his backstory was nominally connected to the vaguely defined Middle East.

There is a case to be made that multidimensional, humanizing representations of characters from a given identity group should include thoughtfully created villains. However, due to the scarcity of notable Latinx supervillains, and even less scholarship on the matter, along with the premise of superheroes serving as icons of morality and aspirational identity, this chapter focuses solely on Latinx superheroes. In the following sections, I position *Latinidad* representation within the context of Marvel and DC superhero narratives, then address the concepts that have become articulated in connection with *Latinidad* in these stories: otherness, sexuality, political issues, labor, culture and ethnicity, and death.

Marvel, DC, and *Latinidad*

First and foremost, it is important to remember that comic books, the birthplace of modern superhero narratives, are commodities. That is not to say that they are not also platforms for creativity, artistic expression, or human connection; rather, it is a reminder that for a character to maintain a presence or for a series to continue, it must sell. So, it is no surprise that publishers often lean on established tropes from other media, such as emphasizing the physical qualities of the characters, their emotional instability, and their need to learn to harness their abilities as opposed to their White counterparts, who are often natural-born leaders and heroes (Aldama, 2017). Creativity and innovation that ethically incorporate marginalized identities may have a moral appeal, but if the comics do not sell, then they will be canceled. As Aldama and Gonzalez (2016) so poignantly express it,

> Simply put, the mainstream DC and Marvel publishers are not interested in innovation—unless it sells. For

> as long as the innovative comic sells, there is money backing its production and distribution. (Of course, this innovative product becomes quickly formulaic when produced in a factory-belt style.) When it stops selling, resources are cut. (p. 15)

There are a variety of reasons why the sales for a given comic book might fail. It could be due to issues with production, changes to the creative team, low advertising efforts, macrolevel economic hardship that causes consumers to buy less, poor story quality, or editorial constraints that limit the ability of creatives to tell their stories the way that they want to, resulting in less resonant narratives. This means that when efforts to increase diversity in terms of character creation and storytelling are made, they are also strategic efforts to widen the appeal of these products to broader audiences (and markets) in addition to the other elements of creating these stories (Millán, 2016). One way that Latinx superheroes have been used to increase diversity without dedicating resources to titles that place them in star roles is to have them appear within ensembles, allowing them to have lines and engage in heroism while still centering more established, typically White, heroes (Frank, 2016). So, for example, DC's Jaime Reyes/Blue Beetle appears as a member of the Teen Titans led by Tim Drake/Robin, or America Chavez joins the Ultimates under the leadership of Carol Danvers/Captain Marvel.

A strategy that comic book publishers employ to maintain the sanctity (read: profitability) of their most recognizable intellectual properties while also experimenting with characters from marginalized backgrounds is to use established monikers in alternative universes/timelines/realities. Doing so allows publishers to try out new characters in prominent roles without disrupting the continuity of their most significant superheroes and suffering the consequences of potentially alienating audiences (Frank, 2016). Perhaps the most high-profile example of this is Marvel's Miles Morales. Morales first debuted in *Ultimate Fallout #4*, which takes place in an alternative universe, and specifically on the planet designated Earth-1610. Stories in this setting are printed under the "Ultimate Marvel" title, as opposed to the mainstream "Marvel" universe, which is the default home of the classic versions of superheroes like Spider-Man, Captain America, Thor, and so on. In the mainstream Marvel universe, the designation for the planet is Earth-616. Miles Morales's origin story involves acquiring powers similar to Spider-Man and then adopting the moniker after the tragic death of that world's first Spider-Man, Peter Parker. Killing off a version of Peter Parker and replacing him with an Afro-Latino middle schooler (Frank, 2016) as Spider-Man was simultaneously controversial and safe. The controversy was that Morales was going to be Spider-Man, albeit not *the* Spider-Man; and the safety of the decision was that because it was in a series that was outside of the mainstream Marvel universe, it could be dismissed as an experiment that could be relegated to the dustbin of comics history if the endeavor failed. In fact, while this was the first time Marvel attempted an Afro-Latino Spider-Man, it was not their first effort at creating a Latino Spider-Man. That distinction belongs to Miguel O'Hara of *Spider-Man 2099*. First published in 1992, Marvel's *2099* series takes place on Earth-928, but whereas Earth-1610 was an alternate universe, Earth-928 is one of multiple possible futures for Earth-616, which effectively makes it an alternate reality. In this version of reality, the world is ruled by megacorporations that have transformed life into a dys-topian nightmare until O'Hara and a group of heroes defeat the villains and usher in a thousand-year era of peace and prosperity (Frank, 2016). This series demonstrates that a major comic book publisher can envision a world where Latinx superheroes are at the forefront of heroic narratives, but only when those stories are told outside of the primary universe's continuity.

Even though the Big 2 publishers have a history of erring on the side of keeping Latinx superheroes in subordinate roles or peripheral titles, this has not always been the case. On occasion, Latinx superheroes are given the spotlight, and while the follow-ing discussion of the articulated constructions of those charac-ters is not a comprehensive account of Latinx superheroes, it does include examples of Latinx characters who have operated in lead roles and on the margins of superhero narratives.

Otherness

In previous chapters in this book, I have discussed how Latinx fig-ures, whether real or fictional, are often framed as different from dominant society in the United States, so much so that we are often conceptualized as personal threats to Americans and exis-tential threats to the nation. Scholars such as Charles Ramirez-Berg (2002) contend that there is a trend within speculative fiction of distorting ethnic identities wherein,

> Hispanics and other immigrant ethnics have become Creatures from Another Planet, Aliens that must be eliminated—either lovingly, by returning them to their native environs (*E.T., Close Encounters of the Third Kind, Harry and the Hendersons, Iceman, Splash, Cocoon*) or

> violently by destroying them (*Alien[s]*, *Predator*, *the Terminator*, *the Aurora Encounter*, *Critters*). (p. 158)

And to be sure, this trend does exist and is very concerning. Yet at the same time, this is not the only way in which otherness is articulated with *Latinidad* in the context of speculative fiction. Superhero narratives are an example of how the genres of science fiction, fantasy, horror, and others can engage with those tropes and create new articulations of *Latinidad*. It is common for Latinx superheroes to be constructed with elements of monstrosity, alienness, and horror-themed qualities, and by doing so, the racialized otherness associated with *Latinidad* becomes an asset rather than a defect (Espinoza, 2016). For example, the previously mentioned character Miguel O'Hara, who acts as the Spider-Man of Marvel's *2099* series, possesses monstrous qualities that also serve as superhero powers. The half-Irish, half-Mexican hero has many of the powers associated with the classic Peter Parker Spider-Man, such as enhanced strength, agility, and durability, but also has venom-secreting fangs that do not retract along with talons that are occasionally retractable (Frank, 2016). In addition to providing abilities that are suited for combat, these physical augmentations are also signs of monstrosity that complicate his ability to pass as a normative human, a clear metaphor for non-White racialization in a White-dominant society. Furthermore, O'Hara's fangs make it difficult for him to speak clearly, which is consistent with the stereotype that Latinxs, particularly immigrants to the United States, are identifiable by their accents.

Of course, other examples are easy to find. The character Jack Russell, who plays the titular character in the Marvel Cinematic Universe (MCU) short-film *Werewolf by Night*, is racialized metaphorically through his lycanthropy. The character is also coded as Latinx through his portrayal by the Mexican actor Gael Garcia Bernal, who speaks with a Spanish-language accent and wears ancestral face paint that evokes an Indigenous aesthetic (Giacchino, 2022). Russell's lycanthropy is framed as a curse but also as an asset, as he uses his werewolf form to liberate himself and others from the clutches of a group of monster hunters intent on ritually killing him and his companions (Giacchino, 2022).

DC's Jaime Reyes, the Blue Beetle, is a Mexican American youth who gained superpowers from a piece of alien technology referred to as the Scarab. The alien hardware granted him powers by fusing with Reyes's body, making it a part of him as opposed to being a piece of gear that could be removed like Batman's suit or Tony Stark's armor. The result is that Reyes was not only granted powers via the advanced alien technology, which he used to help the people in his community on the Mexico-US border, but he was also transformed into a symbol of alienness within the context of American society (Espinoza, 2016). As a racially Brown Latino from El Paso, Texas, he is already heavily associated by connotation with Mexican immigration and implied foreignness. The fusion of the Scarab with his body emphasizes the point by virtue of its extraterrestrial origin.

Marvel's Roberto Reyes serves as another poignant example of how otherness is grafted onto *Latinidad* in a way that inverts stereotypes about Latinxs. This character serves as one of Marvel's Ghost Riders, superheroes and antiheroes who have powers that come from being supernaturally bound to evil spirits. Reyes's powers come from being magically bound to the soul of his deceased uncle Elias Morrow, a satanic serial killer who once owned the car that Reyes now drives, referred to as the Hell Charger. At first glance, Reyes deriving his powers from the condemned soul of a relative who was a professional, violent criminal seems to be another example of the trend of articulating *Latinidad* with criminality. However, Reyes's narrative arc is as a hero who uses his powers to rescue his community from gangs and save the world from galactic-level villains. He is even allowed to join the Avengers. All of this is done while struggling to resist his uncle's influence, and so the trope of criminality as a defining quality of *Latinidad* has been subverted into being an obstacle that is surmounted and compatible with heroism.

Perhaps the most important aspect of the articulation of otherness with *Latinidad* is that it provides a narrative justification for empathy, wherein the heroes are motivated by concern and compassion rather than paternalism. Kobalt, a hero developed by John Rozum and Arvell Jones for Milestone Comics, was a vigilante whose mission was to thwart organized crime. In the final pages of his comic book series, the audience is given clues to his identity, as he is depicted unmasked as a Brown man who goes by the name Miguel. As Frederick Aldama (2009) explains in *Your Brain on Latino Comics*, the implication that Kobalt is Latino helps readers to make sense of the character's narrative arc and personality as the revelation recontextualizes

> his unstated but strongly felt sense of alienation; his deep empathy for the racially victimized and down-and-outs; his deep distaste for underworld kings like Milton St. Cloud and for capitalist ventures like the turning of the barrio into Utopia Park. Perhaps, too, it is this Latino identity that gives him a not-so-superman-like sense of

right and wrong. Kobalt himself often finds himself on the wrong side of the law (p. 46)

From this perspective, the articulation of marginality as a component of *Latinidad* through visual signifiers that indicate mundane otherness within a social context, as well as nonhuman attributes that can also function as superpowers, constructs a vision of Latinx heroism that is community oriented and critically conscious of power structures. These heroes exist on the fringes of society, some going so far as to operate in opposition to the law. As such, they occupy a place within society that is visually signified through extraordinary qualities and that allows them to relate to those that they are rescuing in a way that, I argue, is also an asset for heroism.

Sexuality

The hyperphysicality of superheroes is often visually signified by bodies that are exceedingly muscular, with accentuated physiques that not only connote power but also intense sexuality. As Suzanne Scott (2015) notes, it is normative for superpowered bodies not only to be conceptualized in a way that is easy to sexualize, that is, exaggeratedly muscular men and hourglass-shaped women, but also to be drawn in poses and postures that are reminiscent of pinup art. Latinx characters are not exempt from this treatment. And in keeping with the tradition of heteronormativity within superhero narratives, it is not unusual for Latinx characters to be constructed as heterosexual. For example, DC's Jessica Cruz/Green Lantern has been romantically involved with at least two high-profile heroes: Barry Allen/The Flash (Hitch, 2017) and Bruce Wayne/Batman (Priest, 2019). But what is notable is the articulation of *Latinidad* with queer sexuality. As a group that has often been framed through the lens of alterity, it is not surprising that when comic book publishers have sought to push the boundaries of heteronormativity, they would do so using Latinx heroes since the Latinx community already has an established history within media of being associated with nonnormative sexuality (often hypersexuality or sexual violence). Over the years, there have been quite a few examples of Latinx heroes who have served as symbols for articulating *Latinidad* with sexual orientations beyond the confines of heteronormativity, such as Marvel's Miguel Santos/Living Lightning, who is gay, and Julio Esteban Richter/Rictor, who is bisexual (Aldama, 2009). DC's Carlos Quiñones/Fade is also gay, and in the 1990s, the DC series *The Invisibles* featured a Brazilian trans woman and superhero named Hilde Morales/Lord Fanny (Aldama, 2009). But I would like to draw special attention to four characters in particular because of the way that they reflect varying approaches to depicting *Latinidad* and queerness; those characters are Extraño, Hero Cruz, Renee Montoya, and Miguel Barragan.

One of the earliest forays into articulating queer sexuality with *Latinidad* was DC's Gregorio de la Vega/Extraño ("strange" in Spanish), who debuted in 1988. The character was constructed from a collection of queer stereotypes such as dressing flamboyantly, using effeminate mannerisms, and referring to himself in the third person as "Auntie" (Rodriguez, 2016). The Peruvian hero possessed magic powers, but the mystic arts could not save him from an untimely demise, which will be discussed in the next section related to the articulation of political issues with *Latinidad*. A few years later, in 1997, DC tried again to articulate queer sexuality with *Latinidad* through the character Hero Cruz. Unlike Extraño, Hero was coded in an unmistakable masculine way that would appear to audiences as normatively heterosexual, which made his coming out to his superhero teammate Sparx a shock for her (Rodriguez, 2016). Sparx, a White Canadian woman, had believed herself to be on the precipice of a relationship with the Afro-Puerto Rican hero when he came out to her as gay; she responded with feelings of hurt, betrayal, and rejection (Kesel, 1997a; Kesel, 1997b).

The theme of rejection as an element of narratives related to LGBTQIA+ narratives is not unusual, and in the case of Renee Montoya/The Question, the concept of *Latinidad* became articulated through queer sexuality as well as homophobia. The police officer-turned-vigilante is the daughter of Dominican immigrants who are unaware of her identity as a lesbian until she comes out to them in Gotham Central #10 (Rucka, 2003), a consequence of the villain Two-Face outing her sexual orientation to the public. In the comic issue, she has an off-panel conversation with her extremely religious parents that results in them disowning her, telling her to never return. At another point in the comics, the character is revealed to have had a relationship with a high-profile superhero, Kate Kane/Batwoman (Aldama, 2009). A little more than a decade later, in 2014, DC published a story that stands in stark contrast to Montoya's story of rejection. In their *Teen Titan* series, DC introduced the character Miguel Barragan/Bunker, a gay Latino youth from Mexico, whose experience with community is markedly different from that of Montoya. Barragan is from a small fictional village in Mexico called El Chilar; he is openly gay; he has a boyfriend; and in *Teen Titans* vol. 4 #30, it is made clear that he is a celebrated member of his family and the broader community of El Chilar (Rodriguez, 2016; Lobdell, 2014). As a side note, Bunker's superpower is to create energy constructs with his mind that appear as purple bricks which he shapes into different objects such as walls, fists, or armor. Whether this was done with a specific intention or not, this could be interpreted as being thematic with his queer identity as a reference to the Stonewall riots, a series of protests against law enforcement by the LGBTQIA+ community of New York City that, according to popular myth, involved throwing bricks at police (O'Neill, 2019). Independently the narratives for Montoya and Barragan address the spectrum of lived experiences for LGBTQ+ people within Latinx communities. However, when considered together as conceptual articulations about *Latinidad*, they highlight the reality that homophobia, a product of patriarchy, does not have to be a defining quality of *Latinidad* and opens up new possibilities for conceptualizing queerness within Latinx communities.

Politics

As discussed at the beginning of this chapter, superhero narratives have a long-established history of engaging with political issues. Over the years, Latinx superhero narratives have often been tied to social-cultural concerns within the United States in ways that range from the problematic to the productive. On the more concerning end of the spectrum, there is the troubling articulation between *Latinidad* and criminality. In 1984, the superhero Paco Ramone/Vibe debuted in DC comics as a Puerto Rican gang leader in Detroit (Aldama, 2009). Miguel Santos/Living Lightning first appeared in Marvel comics in 1990. A Latino from

East LA, Santos's narrative involved helping his family with the tumult of his brother having joined one gang and his sister having been killed by another (Aldama, 2009). Angelo Espinosa/Skin, a mutant who was also from East LA, began his superhero journey as a gang member and lost his father to gang violence (Aldama, 2009). DC's Sarah Quiñones/Flashback is depicted as struggling with addiction to crack cocaine, which is a coping mechanism for the trauma of using her powers to save her friends by rewinding time whenever one was mortally wounded (Aldama, 2009). Even though her friends survived, she is still left with the memory of them dying. Each of these stories contains aspects that can be considered humanizing. Ramone, Santos, and Espinosa manage to escape the trappings of gang activity and become superheroes, and Quiñones is eventually able to defeat her addiction. At the same time, it is worth noting that engaging in criminal activity is an idea that is often articulated with *Latinidad*. And while there are positive qualities to these stories, we must consider whether the benefits outweigh the negative representations.

Latinx sexuality has often been conceptualized as a threat to society, whether through predatory sexual violence or the disruption of White American relationships through seduction. One example of how Latinx sexuality has been framed as threatening in superhero narratives was Extraño's death. As previously discussed, Extraño was coded as queer in stereotypical ways, and toward the end of his run in the 1980s, he battled a villain named Hemo-Goblin, who wounded and thus infected Extraño with HIV/AIDS, which resulted in his death soon after (Rodriguez, 2016). This story arc of having a queer Latinx character die from this particular disease during the AIDS epidemic reinforced the problematic idea of HIV/AIDS being a disease that exclusively affected the LGBTQIA+ community. Additionally, because the disease was considered a threat to society and because it was heavily associated with transmission through sexual contact, the story further entrenched the idea that Latinx sexuality posed a threat to the United States. Last, this comic contributed to the misinformation that HIV/AIDS could be spread by mere contact, thus increasing the degree to which Latinx bodies are considered dangerous.

It should come as no surprise that immigration, a political issue that is often framed as a crisis-level threat to the United States, has been articulated to *Latinidad* in superhero narratives. Jaime Reyes/Blue Beetle originally operated in his hometown of El Paso, Texas, a city on the US-Mexico border that is directly opposite Ciudad Juarez, Mexico. The border features prominently in early Reyes's adventures, such as when he discovered that his aunt was exploiting undocumented immigrants (Aldama, 2009); or when he transformed into the Blue Beetle for the first time and woke up in Mexico and had to make his way back across the border (Espinoza, 2016). Immigration also plays a significant role in Marvel's Aña Corazón/Araña's origin story. Her family moved from Mexico City to New York City in order to escape violence (Millán, 2016). This aspect of her story connects her *Latinidad* to immigration as well as to violence in Mexico, which situates Mexico as a place where intense violence occurs, consistent with real-world discourse about Mexican immigration and a part of why Mexican immigrants are considered dangerous.

The articulation of political issues with *Latinidad* is not always negative. A notable example of how political issues have been articulated with *Latinidad* in ways that are ostensibly counter-hegemonic and positive, if at times remarkably ineffective, is that of Miles Morales. To begin, Morales was visually based on the entertainer Donald Glover, but even more so on President Barack Obama (Swift, 2015). It is no coincidence that the first Afro-Latino Spider-Man appeared during the first term of the Obama administration, and is a reflection of the well-established phenomenon that superhero narratives are politically cognizant. Furthermore, Morales's origin story is constructed with political issues at its core. His father, Jefferson Davis, and his uncle, Aaron Davis/Prowler, were street-level criminals in their youth; Jefferson became reformed and left the life of crime, while Aaron advanced to the level of being a professional thief. Morales's family is economically disadvantaged, which is the impetus behind entering into a lottery to attend a prestigious charter school. This aspect of the narrative primes Morales's story to include commentary on the issues of racial oppression and social inequalities related to access to education and economic disparity (Nama and Haddad, 2016). His admittance in the charter school highlights concerns about opportunities for Black and Brown Americans, with the implication that if he had not been admitted, his future would be far less promising (Nama and Haddad, 2016). And yet, in the early days of Morales's stories, there is not much evidence of engagement with these themes beyond their use to set the stage for his origin; they remain present but relatively unexplored. In fact, in the pre-616 adventures of Morales it seems that the biggest indicator of his racial or ethnic identities is his physical appearance as opposed to any other meaningful signifiers of Afro-*Latinidad* (Santos, 2021). After Morales joined the mainstream Marvel universe on Earth-616 (as a result of the multiverse being rebooted in the 2015 comic book event *Secret Wars*), this pattern of keeping the character largely apolitical changed. For example, in the Marvel event *Civil War II*, Iron Man tries to convince Morales to join his side in the new superhero civil war and he frames his position as being opposed to profiling (Bendis, 2016a). Later in the comic book event, Morales has an encounter with the police that reminds him of news stories about unarmed Black men being killed by the police (Bendis, 2016b). It is also during *Civil War II* that Morales grapples with his own capacity for violence, a moment that reflects his cognizance about who he believes himself to be and whether his ancestry determines his future (Bendis, 2016b). This progression over time of the character being used thoughtfully to address issues of racial and ethnic otherness is evidence that there is a capacity within Latinx superhero narratives to engage with political themes in a productive manner.

Labor

Another salient concept articulated with *Latinidad* is that of labor, and in superhero narratives we see many of the same tropes used in film and television applied to Latinx superheroes and their families. Marvel's Angela Del Toro is Hector Ayala's niece and she took up his mantle as the White Tiger after his death. Del Toro worked as an FBI agent (Aldama, 2009), although she eventually leaves the FBI and continues to operate as a vigilante. As discussed earlier, the queer Latina superhero Renee Montoya/ The Question began as a police detective before leaving law enforcement altogether to operate as a vigilante. Articulating official law enforcement with *Latinidad*, as opposed to vigilantism, which is also about the social and moral regulation of deviants, ostensibly positions Latinx characters as guardians of public life. However, when considered in conjunction with the previously addressed articulation of criminality with *Latinidad*, we see that the fuller picture is that we are both the cowboys and the Indians, so to speak, and often only exist relative to structures that regulate bodies of color. At the same time, that both of these characters leave law enforcement to become vigilantes is an implicit condemnation of those organizations and the greater judicial system as being insufficient. If those systems and their agents were able to adequately address the needs of the communities they are supposed to serve, then Montoya and Del Toro wouldn't need to resort to extralegal methods. While not a member of law enforcement, DC's Rafael Sandoval/El Diablo continues the pattern of Latinx superheroes who are official public servants that resort to vigilante methods to do what the government cannot. Sandoval was a city councilman who used the masked vigilante persona of El Diablo to apprehend threats to his community that were beyond his reach as a member of the local government (Jones, 1989). As with Montoya and Del Toro, Sandoval's actions highlight the failure of government to serve marginalized communities, thus articulating the concept of community advocacy to superhero *Latinidad*.

Latinx superheroes are often articulated to other types of labor that are community oriented and typically understood to be low-paying. In *Blue Beetle* comics, Jaime Reyes's father, Alberto, is a mechanic and his mother, Bianca, is a nurse (Aldama, 2009).

In the 2023 film *Blue Beetle*, Reyes takes a job as a house cleaner immediately after graduating college with a political science degree in order to help his family avoid being evicted from their home (Soto, 2023). The jobs held by the Reyes family in the comics and on-screen construct a working-class vision of *Latinidad* that then becomes articulated with heroism through Reyes's adventures. While Miles Morales's primary job as a civilian is being a full-time student, his *Latinidad* becomes articulated to working-class labor through his mother, Rio, who works at a hospital (Bendis, 2013). The creative choice to make Rio Morales a nurse rather than a doctor (or another type of high-earning professional) is consistent with the trend of conceptualizing Latinx labor as working class and thus having limited access to opportunities for significant success, which also connects to the narrative about Miles winning the charter school lottery. The occupation of nursing carries with it the connotation of maternal care, so it is no surprise that the Latina superhero Bonita Juarez/Firebird also has an occupation that is associated with maternal care and community: social worker (Aldama, 2009). However, unlike Rio Morales and Bianca Reyes, Juarez has powers and fights super-powered villains, and thus functions as a symbol that articulates community care, a nurturing disposition, and feminine *Latinidad* with heroism.

Each of the examples provided in this section form articulations between *Latinidad* and working-class labor and in some capacity continue the pattern of conceptualizing Latinx identity as synonymous with economic hardship. There are two notable exceptions, the first is Marvel's Nestor Rodriguez/Eleggua, the leader of the Santerians. In the next section I will discuss the Santerians as symbols of *Latinidad* that have cultural articulations, but in the context of labor, Rodriguez is noteworthy because he deviates from this established pattern. He is a billionaire entrepreneur who works in the entertainment industry (Aldama, 2009). Even though he lives at an economic level far beyond the reaches of the other Latinx characters mentioned in this section, he still operates as a street-level vigilante and serves his community, even going so far as to fight with Daredevil for pushing crime out of the neighborhood of Hell's Kitchen and into Afro-Latinx neighborhoods (Espinoza, 2016). Rodriguez is proof of concept that, while there is value in linking *Latinidad* to working-class labor and struggle, *Latinidad* does not *have* to be linked to that type of labor and social status in order to still be a superhero in service to a Latinx community. The second exception to this pattern is DC's Vibe as he appears in the CW's television series *The Flash*. This version, called Cisco Ramone, is a genius scientist and inventor who serves as the sidekick to Barry Allen/The Flash. This version of Vibe is also Puerto Rican but has no gang affiliations, has led a relatively normal American life, and worked at S.T.A.R. Labs as a mechanical engineer before joining Team Flash. It is his skill as a career scientist that makes him such a valuable asset to the team, and it also illustrates that, like Rodriguez, *Latinidad* can be articulated with heroism and professional success.

Culture and ethnicity

When it comes to overt articulations of *Latinidad* that are meant to signify an ethnic or racialized identity, one of the most easily deployable narrative elements is the use of Spanish. Often, Latinx characters use Spanish words or phrases to signify their

Latinidad, and this is an effective tool for doing so because it can be used throughout dialogue easily and frequently. For example, when Miles Morales meets Miguel O'Hara in *Spider-Man: Across the Spider-Verse*, he greets O'Hara in Spanish and O'Hara responds in kind, thus signifying a shared *Latinidad* (Santos, Powers, and Thompson, 2023). The use of a Spanish surname such as those of the characters discussed in this chapter also evokes a sense of *Latinidad*. Perhaps the most salient example of this is Miles Morales. The creative decision to have his mother keep her original last name rather than take the last name of her husband, Davis, was a decision that normalized the decision for Miles to take his mother's last name. Thus, having him share his father's Black racial identity and his mother's last name immediately signifies Afro-*Latinidad* whether or not the series adds any additional context to elaborate on that identity. In that same vein, a Spanish name can also serve as a point of contention within a narrative that the character has to navigate, as in the case of Aña Corazón. In her series, Corazón struggles with what name to use in her civilian life and as her superhero moniker. Her birth name is Aña, but because her teachers often mispronounce her name as "Ana" when they read it, she instead spells her name as "Anya" to accommodate the English speakers in authority (Millán, 2016). This tension between cultural authenticity and expression of identity versus accommodating the English-speaking hegemony of society in the United States is also reflected in her struggle to decide on a superhero handle. Corazón attempted to use the name Araña for her superhero code name but often encountered the problem of her colleagues calling her Spider-Girl instead (Millán, 2016). Eventually, however, she resists the name Spider-Girl and decides to use the name Araña as an homage to her mother, whose last name was Araña (McGrath, 2007). Doing so also decidedly marks her as a racialized Other in her White-dominant environment as it represents a choice not to assimilate to the English-language hegemony that characterizes her environment.

Another way that superhero stories articulate identity for Latinx characters is through the visual and narrative signifiers of Latin American Indigeneity. To be clear, it is important to draw a distinction between Latin American Indigeneity and *Latinidad*. I am by no means conflating the two by making the assertion that Indigeneity can be used to signify *Latinidad*. Rather, I argue that *Latinidad* is heavily associated with Latin America and that signifiers of Indigeneity (such as clothing, language, and physical features) are one aspect of how Latinxs are racialized as Others within the context of the United States and its media. One way that Indigenous identities are articulated with Latinx characters is through the moniker and costume of a character, such as the hero El Dorado who appeared in the *Super Friends* cartoon in 1977. The character's name is taken from the legendary city of gold that was thought to exist in Latin America; the character also wore an Aztec calendar to reinforce the Indigenous aesthetic (Aldama, 2009). More in-depth articulations of identity for Latinx characters occur in the form of storylines that involve Latin America and its Indigenous Peoples, although it is worth noting that often this is limited to high-profile groups such as the Maya. Both DC's Jaime Reyes and Marvel's Aña Corazón are associated with the Maya, even though Maya Indigeneity is not a component of their personal identities. The Scarab that Reyes uses resided within a Mayan temple in between its initial arrival on Earth and when it bonded with Reyes, thus associating the artifact with a region and people that are connotatively connected to *Latinidad* (Espinoza, 2016). When Aña Corazón joined the Spider Society, a part of her training involved surviving in a wild region in the Yucatan Peninsula (Millán, 2016), a region of Mexico heavily associated with the Maya. Jaime Reyes is of Mexican descent and is from El Paso, Texas, and Aña Corazón was born in Brooklyn and is of Puerto Rican and Mexican descent (Christiansen et al., 2005). Both Mexico and Puerto Rico have Indigenous communities, and yet neither character is specifically identified with one other than these narrative associations with the Maya. And while it is possible that either character could be of Mayan ancestry, or have familial connections to the modern-day Maya, no such articulation has appeared beyond the vague association made within these narratives. But whereas vague Indigeneity is articulated with Reyes and Corazón, the Mayan identity is central to the character K'uk'ulkan/Ch'ah Toh Almehen/Namor in the MCU film *Black Panther: Wakanda Forever* (Coogler, 2022). While the character is clearly constructed as specifically Indigenous Yucatec Mayan, and thus falls outside of the parameters of modern *Latinidad*, the character exists within a superhero narrative as a symbol that articulates Latin American Indigeneity with modern day anti-colonial discourse. This fits within a broader pattern of Latinx activism in the United States that has rhetorically used symbols of Indigeneity to resist the legacies of colonialism in the United States, particularly within former Mexico/the American Southwest (Bebout, 2012).

Closely connected to the theme of Indigeneity is that of religion and worship. *Latinidad* is often connotatively connected to Roman Catholicism, a consequence of the Spanish colonization of parts of Latin America. This connotation is reinforced within superhero narratives when these stories articulate Catholicism with *Latinidad*, as in the case of characters like Bonita Juarez, Rafael Sandoval, and Angelo Espinosa. Juarez is so devoutly Catholic that when she received her powers, she attributed them to divine intervention; Sandoval was trained to box by a Catholic priest; and Espinosa was forced into joining a Catholic youth group by his overprotective Catholic mother in an attempt to keep him from gang activity (Aldama, 2009). Adjacent to this articulation of Roman Catholicism with superhero *Latinidad* is the connection made between the Afro-Caribbean religion of Santeria and the vigilante supergroup: the Santerians. Santeria is a combination of Roman Catholic traditions and West African Yoruba beliefs that formed within the Caribbean; and Marvel's Santerians are a neighborhood vigilante group that have powers associated with the deities of Santeria (Aldama, 2009). This articulation of Santeria with Nestor Rodriguez and the other Latinx characters in the group is an acknowledgment of the diversity of the belief systems within the world of Latinx communities and helps to disrupt the strong connotation of Catholicism with *Latinidad*. If one takes an interpretive approach to the character Aña Corazón and her relationship with her deceased mother, who acts as a guardian of sorts and is connected to Aña's superpowers, then a case can be made that pre-Christian Indigenous beliefs are articulated in her Latina identity (Millán, 2016).

Heroic language

The story at the beginning of this chapter was about a moment where my vocabulary for conceptualizing my identity expanded. Reading comic books and other types of speculative fiction, especially superhero narratives, provided me with tools for understanding how my *Latinidad* situated me as an Other in White-dominant spaces. The characters in these stories were symbols that helped me see differences in general, and *Latinidad* in particular, in a variety of ways that include acknowledging the difficulty and the benefits of an identity which is often framed in a negative light. Through the application of the theory of articulation, I have demonstrated how these symbols are made up of connections that are not inherent and are malleable such that they can be rearticulated in prosocial ways, leaving behind the tired tropes and stereotypes that have plagued depictions of Latinx people for decades. I have also demonstrated that sometimes these burdensome tropes, such as working-class backgrounds and immigration narratives, can be recontextualized as compatible with heroism through stories about superheroes. Thus, these kinds of narratives often have the potential to push back against the kinds of ideological oppression that is often found within other types of media. Ideally, these sorts of stories will continue to propagate provided we see an increase in the number of Latinx creators in positions of power building on the legacies of people like Joe Quesada and Axel Alonso (Aldama and Gonzalez, 2016). With that said, I think it is important to conclude this chapter by looking at a few characters who are, at the time of this writing, opening up new opportunities for Latinxs in superhero narratives: Miles Morales, Jaime Reyes, Namor, and America Chavez.

Miles Morales is perhaps the highest-profile Latinx superhero at the moment. He has been successfully incorporated into the mainstream Marvel Universe/Earth 616 and he has starred in two films, *Spider-Man: Into the Spider-Verse* in 2018 and *Spider-Man: Across the Spider-Verse* in 2023, with a third installment in the series expected in the near future. He has also been adapted into a variety of other media including cartoons and video games, and his momentum does not appear to be ending anytime soon. And yet, there has been remarkably little exploration of his Afro-*Latinidad*; instead, Miles's African-American and Latino identities are treated as relatively the same. As Jorge Santos (2021) argues,

> The thematic structures locate an overlap between African American experience and Latinx experience based in a mutually marginalized status, but these two identities are hardly synonymous—though they are implicitly treated as such. Any tension between them is never expressed, their particulars never explored. (p. 190)

There has been relatively little textual evidence of Miles's bira-cial and bicultural heritage. The comics come close during an early issue when Gloria Morales, Miles's maternal grandmother, blames Miles's difficulties at school on Miles's father's side of the family. This appears to be a nod at the issue of anti-blackness within Latinx cultures, but the accusation is left as an unexplored implication (Santos, 2021). With any luck, we will see Miles's hybrid identity receive more attention and detail so that his Afro-*Latinidad* is made more culturally specific, rather than settling for what appears to be an attempt to make him broadly palatable to a presumed White readership (Santos, 2021).

In 2023, Jaime Reyes appeared for the first time as the star of his own movie, *Blue Beetle*. The character, played by Xolo Mariduena, represents a shift in DC's approach to live-action film adaptations of their comics. Historically, DC has relied heavily on Superman and Batman as their key intellectual properties for film adaptations, with both characters frequently receiving sequels and reboots. Doing so has supported the popular conceptualization of superheroism as being almost exclusively the domain of White heterosexual men. In fact, the iteration of the DC Extended Universe (DCEU) that began with *Man of Steel* in 2013 and ended with *Aquaman and the Lost Kingdom* in 2023, sometimes called the Snyderverse due to the involvement of filmmaker Zack Snyder, centered around Superman and Batman. From this perspective, the DCEU did involve some creative risk choices by deviating from the White, heterosexual, male formula by casting Israeli actress Gal Gadot as Wonder Woman and Hawaiian-American actor Jason Momoa as Aquaman.. It is entirely possible that Reyes could appear in the newly announced DC film universe led by director James Gunn (Klein, 2024), but the manner of that appearance is not guaranteed. Furthermore, it remains to be seen whether this new long-term project and future projects will rely on centering whiteness as previous DC film projects have, or if movies like *Blue Beetle* represent an ideological shift from DC.

In the 2022 film *Black Panther: Wakanda Forever*, the character Namor was incorporated into the MCU. The decision to include Namor was not unusual; the character predates Marvel comics

(Anders et al., 1939) and has been a part of the company from its beginning. What was unusual was the way in which the character was reimagined. Instead of being an Atlantean, a reference to classic Greek mythology, the character was conceptualized as a Yucatan Mayan whose people escaped the horrors of Spanish colonialism. This dramatic change to the character affirms a basic tenet of storytelling that is often overlooked, and which dovetails with the core aspects of articulation: anything can be changed. And while this version of Namor is not Latinx in a strict sense, the character and his narrative arc in the film continue an established tradition of Chicano rhetoric: the utilization of Latin American Indigeneity as a discursive tool to resist the legacies of colonialism (Bebout, 2012). To be clear, this type of rhetoric is not without its problems. My assertion is simply that its symbolic presence within the MCU is significant and could lead to other attempts at normalizing Latin America identity within mainstream superhero narratives.

Last, America Chavez is a character about whom there is relatively little scholarship but who holds great potential for exploring *Latinidad*. The queer Afro-Latina coded superhero with the power to open up portals between universes originally debuted in 2011 and was incorporated into the MCU in the 2022 film *Doctor Strange in the Multiverse of Madness*. The MCU version of the character was portrayed by Xochitl Gomez, thus changing the superhero from being Afro-Latina coded to Mestiza coded, a choice that continues the pattern of reducing Afro-Latinx visibility in media overall. The comic book version of the character's story involves space travel, the coping with trauma through delusions, and an unclear identity beyond being Latina, which leads to why the character is so important: learned *Latinidad* (Planas, 2021). A part of the character's journey in the comics is to find a group to identify with, which leads her to develop a sense of *Latinidad* from Puerto Rican, Colombian, and Tejano cultures, that in turn conveys the sentiment that her sense of *Latinidad* is unstable and developing (Planas, 2021). Melissa C. Planas (2021) argues that this approach to pan-*Latinidad* acts as a commentary on the realities of the Latin American diaspora and how these identities and their hybrid offshoots are becoming increasingly common within the United States. Ideally, in the future we will see this aspect of the comics adapted to the screen provided that Chavez is utilized in future MCU projects. This pan-*Latinidad* aspect of the character underscores a point that is central to this chapter, and indeed this book: there is no singular, exclusively authentic way to represent *Latinidad*. As I have mentioned in other parts of this book, *Latinidad* exists in a *nepantla*, the in-between place, ever fluctuating, shifting, and changing as the borders of *Latinidad* shift and change. Just as these symbols of Latinx heroism are articulated and rearticulated, so too is *Latinidad*, and so like America Chavez , cannot limit ourselves to one singular idea of *Latinidad* to meet the needs of identity con-structed in specific contexts.

6
Virtual *Latinidad*

Manassas, Virginia, 1998

Pitfall Harry Jr., dressed in brown pants, boots, and jacket, runs, jumps, and climbs from platform to platform, searching for his lost father, Pitfall Harry Sr. He scours the remains of an ancient Mayan ruin, evading fire traps, swinging on jungle vines, fighting skeletons, and battling Mayan-themed villains. Deep in the heart of a lush jungle, the noble adventurer pushes farther into the depths of a land filled with wonder and peril, the likes of which no White man has seen before.

Sanford, North Carolina, 2001

Zidane Tribal, a blond-haired, blue-eyed, fair-skinned thief with a monkey tail, stands face-to-face with his companions against Necron, an eternal avatar of the concept of death. This embodied aspect of reality has no chance against this particular rogue and his plucky company of misfits, mages, and mercenaries. Soon, Necron will admit defeat and the motley band of unlikely heroes will return home, triumphant in having saved the universe.

Reidsville, North Carolina, 2003

Master Chief Petty Officer John-117 barrels his way through an alien labyrinth in a far-away galaxy, as grotesque, tentacled monstrosities relentlessly pursue him. The supersoldier is a product of the special forces program code-named SPARTAN-II, developed by the United Nations Space Command to be an efficient weapon of war against human terrorist organizations. He was not made to fight alien forces that pose existential threats to humanity, but he is equal to the task. The energy shield of his Mark IV MJOLNIR power armor crackles and pops as small, bulbous, squid-like creatures hurl themselves at him, hoping to make contact with his pale flesh and begin the process of transforming him into one of the Flood, only to explode upon contact with the shield. Ahead of him the supersoldier can see several fleshy horrors lumbering toward him, composed of awkward limbs, tentacles, and the lifeless, once-human faces that have been trapped in a moment of perpetual agony, a silent scream. He reloads his shotgun as he sprints and closes the gap. He will not be stopped.

Wentworth, North Carolina, 2006

Link, a fair-featured young warrior wielding a sword and shield, squares off with the Dark Lord Gannondorf. The two stand in a desolate field under a dark, angry sky, surrounded by a magical barrier summoned by the evil sorcerer. The imperious villain is styled in an Orientalist manner with dark skin, a prominent hooked nose, a beard, and elaborate jewelry that matches his equally elaborate armor and flowing cape. This is but one of many "final battles" between these two figures, a cycle that has played out time and time again throughout the narrative world's past and future. And as ever, the hero will be victorious.

Bowling Green, Ohio, 2015

Talion, a Ranger of Gondor and a captain of the occupying army that once held the Black Gate, stalks the hellscape that is Mordor as a wraith. He is not remarkable in his appearance, sharing the fair skin and dark hair of most of his countrymen; and while he was formidable when he was alive, his skill was not enough to save his family or himself from being slaughtered by the forces of the enemy. But, as a vengeful spirit bound to the soul of the long-dead elf Celebrimbor, he has become a force to be reckoned with. Behind him marches an army of Uruks and dozens of orc captains he has bent to his will through magical means, their glowing eyes a sign of Talion's domination. They are marching to the Black Gate, where Talion was ritually sacrificed, to slay the Black Hand, a powerful sorcerer in service to the Dark Lord Sauron. Talion is swift, he is terrible, and before his story is through, he will be the nightmare that haunts monsters.

In video games you can live a thousand lives as a thousand heroes, you can save worlds in alien galaxies and spit in the face of the masters of Hell, and all you have to do is agree to be White.

Press start to begin

Each of the games that I just described, in order, *Pitfall: The Mayan Adventure*, *Final Fantasy IX*, *Halo: Combat Evolved*, *The Legend of Zelda: Twilight Princess*, and *Middle-Earth: Shadow of Mordor*, are games that I devoted countless hours to from the age of 10 to 26, and generally represent the types of games that I have been playing since I was five years old. These games are also representative of the dominant trends within the video game industry: action-adventure, role-playing, and first-person shooter games that feature White male protagonists as the primary playable characters. My experience is far from unique. Historically, playable characters in video games have overwhelmingly been White men, and normatively presumed to be heterosexual (Gray and Leonard, 2018). Interestingly, of the characters that I described in the previous section, the only one that was not obviously depicted as White was John-117/Master Chief, and for many years he was not obviously racialized. The only identity markers were his name, rank, species, voice, and apparent gender. His race was never visibly identified because he was never depicted outside of his armor. However, the live action television adaptation of the *Halo* franchise depicts the Master Chief as White in the pilot episode of the series (Killen, Kane, and Bathurst, 2022), thus removing the racial ambiguity of the character and reinforcing the idea that in the absence of any clear racialization, whiteness is presumed to be the default.

In 2023, the video game industry generated $47.3 billion in the United States and $184 billion globally (Wijman, 2024). According to the Entertainment Software Association, 61 percent of people in the United States play video games (Entertainment Software Association, 2024). Video game players range in age from 5 to 90 years old, with the 47 percent being between the ages of 18 and 50 years old (Entertainment Software Association, 2024). In terms of adult video game players, White Americans make up 75 percent of players, 19 percent are Hispanic, 12 percent are Black/African Americans, Asian and Pacific Islanders make up

4 percent, and Native American/Alaskan players make up 3 percent (Entertainment Software Association, 2024) (note: the survey for this report allowed for selecting multiple racial and ethnic identities). Roughly 46 percent of video game players are women and approximately 53 percent are men, with around 1 percent identifying otherwise or opting to not identify in the generated report (Entertainment Software Association, 2024). Seventy-eight percent of households in the United States have played a video game in the last 12 months (2023–2024), which means that a large number of people who may not play games are still exposed to them in some capacity (Entertainment Software Association, 2024). With such a pervasive presence among the various demographic groups in the United States, and the clear force of presence that the industry has in the domestic and global economy, it is clear that video games are here to stay. This is all the more reason to consider how video games, like other forms of media, play a role in shaping the racial identities of Latinx people.

In the following sections of this chapter, I will discuss how video games function as persuasive artifacts that are unique in their relationship to the audience compared to the other forms of media addressed in this book. I will begin by addressing a few key concepts and approaches to understanding video games as persuasive media that reproduce ideologies of race. Then, I will discuss the relationship between video games and race and ethnicity in general, and then proceed to discuss how video games have engaged with the concept of *Latinidad* in particular. I will conclude the chapter by engaging with video games as a form of media that holds real potential for positively affecting identity development and the collective social imagination.

Bordered gamescapes

> To play video games is to engage with the myths of a constituency whose access, agency and ability to wield the technology allows them to communicate their wishes, fears, dreams—and even identity politics— through a form of interactive entertainment. Games differ from theatre, film or television; but they do operate as expressions of the "dream life" of a culture, whose playable depths are only beginning to be plumbed. (Murray, 2018, p. 3)

These remarks from Soraya Murray, from the book *On Video Games: The Visual Politics of Race, Gender, and Space*, gets at the heart of what makes video games compelling both as a form of entertainment and an artifact for examination. While the medium does not have the established longevity of television, film, news broadcasts, or superhero narratives, it is nonetheless a powerful medium for disseminating ideas in a way that is unique. Whereas the other mediums mentioned tell a story to the audience, video games build a story *with* the audience in ways that allow players to express their dreams, fears, and identities to varying degrees depending on the options afforded by the particular game. Even interactive stories like the film *Black Mirror: Bandersnatch* (2018) fall short in this capacity, because while they do allow the audience to make choices and thus shape the narrative, they are still not engaging in acting out the protagonist's role the way that a player does in a video game. The degree to which a player can shape a game's story through character choices varies greatly depending on the game, but even in the earliest days of gaming, the option of succeeding or failing to win served as a unique method of co-constructing the narrative.

As discussed in other parts of this book, depictions of *Latinidad* in mass media are manifestations of power that inform society's conceptualization of those who fall within the category of *Latinidad*. In the context of video games, ordinary, illustrated representation becomes playable representation (Murray, 2018), which not only speaks to the interactivity that characterizes the medium, but also situates the player as a participant with agency in depicting that representation, whether that is in the form of choices that are made in the game or even in deciding to play the game at all. From the perspective of video games as ideological artifacts that contribute to the social imagination, the settings, worlds, and landscapes of video games become sites for addressing real-world concerns (Murray, 2018). It is not enough for gamescapes to be vivid, state-of-the-art demonstrations of technology, or immersive. They must make sense. The intersecting components of the world and its mechanics must seem natural to the point of being inevitable, as though these works of fiction could have only ever looked as they do (Murray, 2018).

To make sense of how games function as persuasive vehicles for ideologies, we need conceptual frameworks for grappling with this unique medium. I have selected two frameworks for doing so: procedural rhetoric, developed by Ian Bogost, and C.G.K. Gonzalez's conceptualization of video games as borderlands. I will begin by discussing procedural rhetoric and then connect that concept to the idea of video games as borderlands.

Bogost's (2007) concept of procedural rhetoric positions video games as systems that function to achieve a persuasive goal through computational processes. In the book *Persuasive Games: The Expressive Power of Video Games*, Bogost (2007) argues that it is not sufficient to examine the visual or narrative components of a game in order to understand its persuasive power. Rather, the visual and narrative elements must be considered in conjunction with the rules and mechanics of the game when those processes endorse a discernible rhetorical vision. For example, Tom Grimwood (2018) applies procedural rhetoric to address how the concept of madness is framed within specific video games, not just in terms of how madness is represented narratively but also in terms of how madness becomes a game mechanism that affects gameplay. One cultural production that Grimwood (2018) examines is the game *The Suffering* (2004), which features a mechanic where the player character's madness is measured on a meter and a sufficiently high level of madness allows the character to transform into a monster. Playing the game in the form of a monster does not just affect navigating the game and fighting enemies; the amount of time spent as a monster is also a factor the game software uses to determine whether the player qualifies for the good, bad, or neutral ending of the story (Grimwood, 2018). The more time spent as the monster, the more likely the conclusion of the story will be the "bad" ending wherein the player character is revealed to have murdered his family; thus, the game mechanic acts persuasively to facilitate a rhetorical vision that connects mental health to violent criminality (Grimwood, 2018). Each aspect of a video game, such as the visual elements, narrative, gameplay mechanics, character con-structions, and so on, are considered unit operations, which are in essence computational processes that are interwoven with each other (Bogost, 2007). Bogost's (2007) assertion is not that these unit operations are realistic in their representativeness; rather, they are abstract representations of real-world concepts that are used to form particular rhetorical arguments about how the world could or should work.

There are two salient reasons for using procedural rhetoric to con-ceptualize video games for the purpose of this chapter. The first is that it allows us to think of video games as systems comprised of interdependent processes that can operate within a given set of ideological constraints such that it is either hegemonic or counter-hegemonic. Doing so helps us to consider what those interdependent processes are, how they facilitate a given mode of reasoning, and how they are ideologically value-laden. We will return to this approach in the section on *Latinidad* in video games. The second reason for taking this systems approach to video game analysis is that framing games as systems with which we interact lends itself to understanding games as constructed worlds that we occupy when we choose to play them. This con-nects to the Gonzalez's approach to seeing video games as bor-derlands. Gonzalez (2023) asserts that, similar to how Anzaldua articulates border culture as being both inside and outside of two different cultural systems, so too is a video game player both inside and outside of the video game as they guide a character through the game. González (2023) further argues that the act of crossing into the coded software of the game is analogous to crossing a geopolitical border, and that learning to adapt to the rules and programming of the game is conceptually similar to integrating into a cultural system.

According to González (2023), the act of playing a game requires that a person step into a designed identity. The concept of a designed identity was coined by Shira Chess (2017) and it refers to how the player is conceptualized by the video game industry. In effect, the video game industry as a whole constructs an ideal target audience that it attempts to appeal to through advertising and game design. This imaginary video game player that has been constructed by the industry is a White young man who is heterosexual, cisgendered, able bodied, and middle-class. Chess (2017) designates this imagined gamer as Player One. Player One is the target consumer to whom major video game companies try to appeal. Chess (2017) takes this a step further and asserts that Player Two is a fictional consumer designed by the industry to target women and girls. Both Player One and Player Two are constructs, warped depictions of who the industry *thinks* they are trying to appeal to, when in reality they are designing identities that players have to occupy at least in part in order to play a given game. González (2023) adds onto this way of thinking about player subjectivity by introducing Player Juan. If Players One and Two are by-products of the video game industry attempting to appeal to idealized men and women consumers, then Player Juan is a discursive formation constructed through the use of long-established stereotypes and tropes about Latinx communities (González, 2023). Player Juan is who the video game industry thinks we are, and the details of that conceptualization are made evident in how Latinx people are depicted (or not) within video games. In order to understand how video games construct Player Juan through in-game constructions of *Latinidad* we first have to understand the centrality of whiteness in games and how race in general has been represented within these virtual worlds.

Digitized race

The 2009 article "The Virtual Census: Representations of Gender, Race and Age in Video Games," by Williams, Martins, Consalvo, and Ivory, discusses in detail a study conducted by the researchers wherein they analyzed the primary (player) and secondary (non-player) characters in 150 of the best-selling video games from March of 2005 to February 2009. The study involved a demographic analysis of the characters in terms of race/ethnicity and gender. The researchers found that 80.05 percent of all characters, primary and otherwise, were White (Williams et al., 2009). The percentages of non-White characters by category were: 10.74 percent Black; 2.71 percent Hispanic; 1.39 percent biracial; .09 percent Native American; and 5.03 percent Asian/Pacific Islander (Williams et al., 2009). For perspective, the percentages of the population of the United States by race/ethnicity for that time frame were as follows: 75.1 percent White; 12.3 percent Black; 12.5 percent Hispanic; 2.4 percent biracial; .9 percent Native American; 4 percent Asian/Pacific Islander. White Americans and Asian/Pacific Islander Americans were overrepresented, and all other categories were significantly underrepresented. Williams et al. (2009) also found that 84.95 percent of primary characters were White; 9.67 percent were Black; 3.69 percent were biracial; and 1.69 percent were Asian/Pacific Islander. Hispanics and Native Americans did not appear as primary characters, only secondary characters. This same study found that men were 89.55 percent of the primary characters and 85.47 percent of the secondary characters, whereas women were 10.45 percent of the primary characters and 14.65 percent of the secondary characters (Williams et al., 2009). While not explicitly mentioned, it is reasonable to assume that all of these characters were cis-gendered. The data reveals that at the time, White masculinity was central to video game narratives and by extension closely associated with the mechanics of being a player character. The data also reveals a hierarchy of racialized identities, wherein all non-White masculine identities are subordinated, and in the case of Latinx and Native American player characters, erased entirely.

More than a decade after the publication of the Williams et al. (2009) study, it seems that things have only slightly improved. A study conducted by Diamond Lobby, a video game review company, examined 100 games published between 2017 and 2021 (Lin, 2023). The study involved race and gender analyses of characters with preset identities (as opposed to games where the character's race and gender is customizable) that were also human (excluding animals, aliens, monsters, etc.). A total of 79.2 percent of the main protagonists were male and 20.8 percent were female; 66.5 percent of all characters were male, 27.7 percent were female, and 5.8 were non-binary or had no documented gender (Lin, 2023). The report identified 61.2 percent of all characters as White and 38.8 percent as Non-White; 54.2 percent of all main characters were identified as White (Lin, 2023). The study used a White/non-White binary of categorization due to the lack of sufficient information in the games to identify the race and ethnic identities of the non-White characters. Interestingly, the study found that 9.5 percent of all the games reviewed had only White playable characters and 5.3 percent of the games had no White playable characters (Lin, 2023).

These studies indicate that there has been a discernible shift in the number of non-White characters depicted on-screen, which is ostensibly progressive if for no other reason than because this means that non-White player characters are becoming more prevalent. However, this is not a reflection of the quality of those depictions. Historically, depictions of non-White American racial and ethnic groups within video games have relied on stereotypes and tropes that have been well established in other mediums, particularly film, television, and print. As such, video games are spaces where players engage with discourses and ideologies related to race and participate in their construction through interaction (Leonard, 2003). In his 2003 article "'Live in Your World, Play in Ours': Race, Video Games, and Consuming the Other," researcher David Leonard (2003) asserts that the game *Grand Theft Auto III* reflects the centrality of whiteness in video games and thus endorses the ideology of the superiority of whiteness. He writes,

> *GTA III* legitimizes white supremacy and patriarchy and privileges whiteness and male-ness, all the while substantiating the necessity of law and order and reactionary social governance. You, as the only white character, are sent to Liberty City to lead and/or control the other. (Leonard, 2003, p. 3)

The non-White bodies in *GTA III* are framed as dangerous in addition to being deeply intertwined with unemployment, poverty, crime, and violence, all of which serves as the justification for the White player character's actions and by extension justifies White hegemony (Leonard, 2003). Scholars Burgess, Dill, Stermer, Burgess, and Brown (2011) echo this sentiment, arguing that not only are stereotypes a central element to the character construction of non-White characters, but their underrepresentation is a part of how the stories are told.

When minority characters are depicted, the stereotypes used to construct their characters are often recycled from other media. For example, Black Americans are often heavily associated with criminality, athletics, or the supernatural, and Asian characters are likely to appear as martial arts experts (Dickerman, Christensen, and Kerl-McClain, 2008, p. 25). Native Americans are often depicted as inclined toward violence and adorned with items like feathers and paint that have become pan-Indian signifiers (Carpenter, 2021; Valdez, 2024). But this is not to say that there has not been significant progress in the area of racialized character construction. We are a long way from the days of games like *Custer's Revenge*, an Atari game made in 1982 where the goal was to play as Lt. Colonel George A. Custer and dodge arrows so that he could rape a Native American woman (Dickerman, Christensen, and Kerl-McClain, 2008). However, the fact that the game was ever made and published speaks to the origins of gaming.

Fortunately, the increase in racial and ethnic representation as indicated in the Diamond Lobby report (Lin, 2023) has been accompanied by more developed depictions of characters of color. Unfortunately, that has not stopped mainstream game publishers from finding other ways to subordinate their identities. As TreaAndrea M. Russworm (2017) points out in her analysis of the video games *The Last of Us* and *The Walking Dead*, the mere presence of characters of color, in this instance Black characters, "satisfies an uncritical multiculturalist imperative to merely include diverse characterizations in game world" (p. 112). Russworm's (2017) contention is that while the Black characters in *The Last of Us* and *The Walking Dead* video games have spoken dialogue, plot relevance, and in at least one instance emotional depth, the characters are still killed off, and thus blackness maintains its role as a visual signifier of suffering. Gray and Leonard (2018) refer to this pattern of Black and Brown characters being designed to die as Black Death. They point to the game *Battlefield 1* as an exemplar of this phenomenon as the game features two members of the historical Harlem Hellfighters, a US military regiment of predominantly African American and Puerto Rican men who served in World War I, as playable characters. Both characters die violently, making the deaths of these characters aspects of the game's spectacle (Gray and Leonard, 2018). Gray and Leonard (2018) thoughtfully articulate this aspect of the game as in keeping with the established tradition of subordinating non-White racial identities. They write,

> Gaming imagines a world of good and evil, of domination and annihilation, where whiteness and American manhood characterize protectors and heroes—values not afforded the pixelated Harlem Hellfighters in *Battlefield 1*. In this way, games provide a training ground for the consumption of narratives and stereotypes as well as opportunities to become instruments of hegemony; they offer spaces of white male play and pleasures, and

> create a virtual and lived reality where white maleness
> is empowered to police and criminalize the Other. (Gray
> and Leonard, 2018, p. 6)

Their framing of video games as a kind of reality connects to Gonzalez's idea that video games can be seen as borderlands where the inside of the virtual world and the outside of the player's world converge. In the next section I will discuss how *Latinidad* is constructed within the virtual borderland.

Virtual *Latinidad*

A critical aspect of understanding how *Latinidad* is constructed within video games is the fact that often it is not. As González (2023) notes, it is peculiar that we are significantly underrepresented in video games even though those identified as Hispanic by the US census account for 16.3 percent of the population; the second-largest ethnic group, with White Americans identified as the largest (US Census Bureau, 2021). This noticeable absence sends the message that *Latinidad* is incompatible with heroism and protagonist positioning without certain constraints and narrative elements, which we will discuss in further detail later in this section. First, let us begin by discussing the ways in which *Latinidad* is most commonly constructed in video games.

Phillip Penix-Tadsen (2013) uses three categories for organizing how *Latinidad* is represented in video games that have in-game connections to Latin America: Contras, Tomb Raiders, and *Luchadores*. Games that fall under the category of Contras (named for the game *Contras* on the Nintendo Entertainment System) are those that feature Latin American cultures closely associated with military/paramilitary warfare such as the 2013 game *Call of Duty: Modern Warfare 2* and the remastered version released in 2020, as well as a host of other combat-oriented games (Penix-Tadsen, 2013). These types of games often deal in heavy-handed tropes and stereotypes about revolutionary or drug-cartel related conflicts within Latin America and feature a character from a Western (read: White) country killing Latin Americans to accomplish an objective.

The second category, Tomb Raiders, includes games that use Latin American locations as the settings for adventurers who are typically White and often men (Penix-Tadsen, 2013). One notable adventurer is Lara Croft of the *Tomb Raider* franchise, for whom this category was named. As an interesting sidenote, Lara Croft, a British explorer, was originally designed as a South American adventurer named Laura Cruz but was redesigned to appeal to US gamers (González, 2023). Games in this category are set in Central and South America and utilize images that clearly signify ancient Indigenous cultures, such as the Mayan, Aztec, or Incan civilizations, or wilderness settings that may also include depictions of Indigenous Peoples. Such settings were popular in the early generations of video games, such as *Pitfall: The Mayan Adventure* (1994) and *The Mask of the Sun* (1982), and continue to be popular in modern video games such as the *Uncharted* franchise, which used South American settings multiple times. These settings are constructed in a way that emphasizes themes of danger, exoticism, and the mysterious, all of which are in stark contrast to the protagonist who is usually constructed as familiar and knowable because of the cultural reference point of a White adventurer who is deeply entrenched in our media. These types of games reduce rich, complex histories and cultures to game elements designed to show how adept the protagonist is at navigating and ultimately triumphing over the perilous unknown.

The last category, *Luchadores*, is reserved for two types of games: those that use actual depictions of Mexican masked wrestlers, *luchadores*, which literally translates to fighters, and those games that struggle, *lucha*, against stereotypes in favor of complex, nuanced, and multidimensional depictions of Latin Americans (Penix-Tadsen, 2013). As with the other two categories, this category's name is a reference to a particular video game: *Lucha Libre AAA: Héroes del Ring*, a Spanish-language game that culturally situated Mexican wrestling by addressing its history and includes biographical information about real-life *luchadores* (Penix-Tadsen, 2013). This game reflects an intentional effort to humanize a sport that, at least in the context of the United States, is often reduced to a punch line or a gimmick for American audiences. Penix-Tadsen extends this concept of games that struggle against stereotypes to other games that are popular in the United States such as *Red Dead Redemption* (2010). He argues that the game's narrative involving the Mexican Revolution and the dimensionality of the non-player characters add depth to the depictions that illustrates a "deeply contextualized moral relativism that eliminates the 'us versus them' mentality and produces a world in which nobody is right" (Penix-Tadsen, 2013, p. 184).

From González's (2023) perspective that playing a game is an act of virtual immigration, we are then crossing into a world that is often dehumanizing, wherein Player Juan is designed as a two-dimensional identity that is constructed from oppressive tropes and stereotypes. Penix-Tadsen's (2013) categorization of how Latin America is represented in video games does not, strictly

speaking, include representations of how *Latinidad* is represented in games where the story takes place in the United States.
However, it is clear that the organizing principle that he developed can be applied. US-based Latinx gangsters and criminals
like those depicted in the *Grand Theft Auto* franchise fit easily into
the Contras category. Instead of the jungles and ancient ruins of
South America, the Tomb Raiders category could be adapted to
include the American Old West, as depicted in the *Call of Juarez*
and *Red Dead* franchises. But if there is any hope for Player Juan
to progress from two- to three-dimensional, then it resides in the
third category of *Luchadores* games that resist stereotypes.

In his book *Ready Player Juan: Latinx Masculinities and Stereotypes
in Video Games*, C. G. K. González (2023) discusses constructions
of *Latinidad* that fit into the *Luchadores* category. In particular,
he goes in-depth on the Marvel superhero Miles Morales/Spider-
Man as he appears in the video games *Marvel's Spider-Man*
(2018) and *Marvel's Spider-Man: Miles Morales* (2020), as well as
the characters Sean and Daniel Diaz of the game *Life is Strange
2*. According to González (2023), these characters push back
against stereotypes that are often associated with Latinx characters. In the case of Miles Morales, his stand-alone game released
in 2022 is textured with some cultural references to Puerto Rican
language, music, and tradition, but only some. González (2023)
notes that these references are entirely absent from *Marvel's
Spider-Man* (2018), where the character is introduced, and in
his own game the references are fairly infrequent. Additionally,
Morales's heroism pushes back against the vilification of Latinxs
often seen in video games, but his heroism exists relative to the
original Spider-Man, Peter Parker, and thus whiteness. González

(2023) asserts that *Life is Strange 2* also deeply humanizes Latinxs, in this case two Mexican American brothers who are attempting to escape to Mexico after the murder of their father. While the game depicts a loving and protective relationship between Sean and Daniel, and even allows for the possibility of Sean to engage in a same-sex relationship with another homeless youth, Finn, the game is still characterized by pervasive whiteness. González (2023) argues that the game's engagement with Make America Great Again political themes, often in the form of racism and bigotry directed at the Latinx main characters, reinforces the idea that Latinx stories have to exist relative to dominant discourses in American politics that involve demonizing Latinx communities. Furthermore, González (2023) contends, the narrative structure of the game, the events, and the character choices are often dependent on the whiteness of many of the characters, such as White characters being able to engage in criminal activity without repercussion. In effect, without whiteness, the events of the game would violate the suspension of disbelief.

Penix-Tadsen's and González's work paints a complicated picture of *Latinidad* in gaming. Clearly, bigoted ideologies are central to the representation of Latinx communities in video games, and yet there is possibility for improvement. In the final section of this chapter, I will address that possibility and discuss how video games as sites of ideological formation can be used productively through a concept that González (2023) calls digital *mestizaje*.

Digital mestizaje

Everett and Watkins (2008) describe video games as racialized pedagogical zones because of the way that video games teach not only entrenched ideologies of race and racism, but also how game play's pleasure principles of mastery, winning, and skills development are often inextricably tied to and defined by familiar racial and ethnic stereotypes. (p. 150)

This is consistent with Soraya Murray's (2018) assertion that video games are cultural productions that contribute to social imagination as they also engage with real-world concerns surrounding ideologies of identity. Bogost's (2007) concept of procedural rhetoric underscores this point as this approach situates video games as more than mere sites of discourse but as persuasive tools that endorse a given ideological message. While real-world race and ethnic identities are rarely incorporated into game mechanics, with the exception of a game like *South Park: The Fractured But Whole* where adjusting the game's difficulty setting also affects the player character's skin color (easy = fair skin, very difficult = dark skin), the use of racialized identities and aesthetics function as operation units that contribute to the system processes of a given game. As a sidenote, it is common in fantasy video games for race to be explicitly gamified, granting bonuses and abilities that affect gameplay, but as of yet, that is not a common occurrence in games rooted in real-world settings.

If we operate with the understanding that video games are persuasive artifacts that attempt to influence players' perspectives on race and racism as it exists in society, and if we understand that Player Juan is an invention of the video game industry that conceptualizes Latinx players as people with whom these tropes, stereotypes, and clichés would resonate, then it seems that there is little hope for counter-hegemonic, humanizing identity development for Latinxs through video games. But that is not the case for two reasons. The first is that, as Penix-Tadsen argues in his book *Cultural Code: Video Games and Latin America* (2016), the visual representations of *Latinidad* in video games operate in a semiotic capacity, meaning that the visual elements of the game are open to multiple, even conflicting, interpretations. Penix-Tadsen (2016) also argues that the already unstable relationship between a sign and the meaning attached to it is made even more dynamic due to the element of interactivity in video games. Since players can interact with certain elements within the game, the player also has the option to renegotiate the meaning attached to a particular sign. Thus, a cowboy's firearm does not have to be a symbol of wanton violence. The player can wield the weapon in the defense of the poor and oppressed and transform the weapon into a symbol of justice. The second reason there is potential for prosocial identity development is the concept that González (2023) calls digital *mestizaje*. According to González (2023), this is the idea that through interaction with digital media that constructs *Latinidad* in a particular way, whether positively or negatively, a Latinx consumer has the opportunity to engage critically with the artifact and reflect on the complexities of their own lived experience with *Latinidad* in comparison with the media they are consuming.

This approach to engaging with depictions of *Latinidad* within video games asks us to recognize the reductive nature of many representations of Latinx people. One such point of critical reflection would be to inquire about those who are seldom depicted, if at all, such as women, queer, transgender, and other gender nonconforming people who exist within Latinx communities.

Almost all of the research here that engages with representations of Latinx people focuses on men, and that is because there has been very little research done on people with non-male gender identities, which is largely attributable to the absence or lack of prominence of non-male characters in video games.

González (2023) positions video games as borderlands where the virtual world intersects with the real world of the player, forming a *nepantla* space as articulated by Anzaldua. When I played the games that I described at the start of this chapter, unbeknownst to myself, I occupied that *nepantla*. Previously, I discussed how I developed a sense of internalized racism through the media that I consumed, and my relationship with video games fostered that sentiment. The games I played did not depict *Latinidad* in a stereotypical manner, or in any way for that matter. But as racialized pedagogical zones, they reinforced the idea that bravery and heroism are connected to whiteness exclusively, and so I leaned into that albeit unconsciously. By the time I was an adult in my twenties, I had learned that *Latinidad* was tantamount to criminality, violence, and predatory behavior through the news, film, and television that I consumed. There were precious few examples of *Latinidad* connected to heroism for me to consume, but as I have discussed in this chapter, there was an abundance of White heroes in video games to capture my imagination. And all I had to do to reconcile my own identity with theirs was to be as White as I could be, in my speech, in my mannerisms, my interests, and my imagination.

7
Suturing together Pocho Villa

I like to joke that I am a racial Rorschach test, that when people look at me, they have to decide what they see. I can pass as White, but in my experience when I am engaging with non-Latinx folks and I mention being Mexican American, the most common response is something along the lines of "yeah, I thought you were something like that." I have come to expect those sorts of remarks, and honestly, they are better than when folks ask, "what are you?" or assume I do not speak English. My skin is light brown, like maybe I am a White guy who can tan, but my black (now going gray) hair, brown eyes, and broad facial features usually signify that I am not *quite* White. In truth, I resemble both the Brown mestizo *Norteño* Mexican and the European White American sides of my family. When I am with either group, I look like I can fit in easily, like I belong.

I will admit, though, there have been times when I tried to pass as White. In my youth into my early 20s I waffled between trying to express a sense of *Latinidad* that I was comfortable with and increasing my proximity to whiteness, leaning into speech, mannerisms, attire, and popular culture associated with dominant society, especially fantasy and science fiction. Now that I am in my mid-30s, I still try to pass as White when I get pulled over by the police by emphasizing my North Carolina accent just a little bit. As of this writing, some counties in North Carolina have a 287(g) program that authorizes local law enforcement to operate as immigration enforcement (US Immigration and Customs Enforcement, n.d.), and in my hometown the police have been known to wait outside of the local Catholic church in their patrol cars and profile people leaving the Spanish mass to try to catch folks driving without a license so they can issue them a ticket. So, I try to pass to avoid being profiled. But, starting sometime in my late 20s, I no longer felt the need to try to pass in my daily life and instead I finally began to develop a sense of *Latinidad* that I felt fit me. That was a choice, as much as trying to pass was a choice. As I wrap up this book, the concept of "choice" is going to be central.

Of *nepantla* and "becoming"

Ultimately, for me, *Latinidad* is about making decisions. My birth father chose to leave me for another life, another family, by the time I was five, and so I decided to reject being Mexican for most of my early life. This did not really change until my dad adopted me when he married my mom, and so gradually I became open to *Latinidad*. When it was just my mother and I living in Virginia, she often took me to the Smithsonian museums in DC, and I remember on one particular occasion we came across an exhibit that depicted the Indigenous Peoples of the Southwestern United States and northern Mexico. She told me, "these are the people you come from, the people your *abuelos* (grandparents) come from, there is a lot to be proud of." She tried to develop my sense of *Latinidad* through speaking Spanish, exposing me to the music, culture, food, traditions, and people, but at best I chose only to half-listen and often not at all. The cracks in the foundation of my self-concept that came from my rejection of *Latinidad* provided opportunities for the mass media to whisper messages of whiteness in my ear, and for a long time I chose to listen to those. In this chapter I am going to review and discuss the salient themes addressed in this book, ask some relevant questions that are meant to spark reflection and inquiry, and grapple with the concept of *Latinidad* and the term "Latinx." I will begin by reviewing the academic toolbox, racialized ethnicity, *nepantla*, and the concept of suturing identity that was discussed in chapter 1. Then I will discuss the idea of learning *Latinidad* through mass media as it relates to the forms of media that I have discussed in this book. After that, I will pick apart and trouble the concept of *Latinidad*, and then conclude by considering how to move forward as Latinx people in the United States. In order to understand the decisions that one must make to navigate *Latinidad*, we must first recognize the structures that limit and inform our choices. Whether a Latinx person is born in the United States or arrives here as a child or adult, they enter into a system of racialization that is beyond their control, wherein being ethnically of Latin American origin or descent places them in proximity to the racial category of brownness in a way that does not occur for those who occupy a White, of European descent, positionality in the racial hierarchy. To exist in the United States at all is to occupy an environment that is ordered as a hierarchy which places individuals and groups into racialized spaces/positions (Bonilla-Silva, 2015); and while some individuals may be able to enter and exit those spaces due to the fluidity of interpersonal perceptions of race, many people cannot and doing so does not change the racial structure.

Understanding that the racial hierarchy is a fundamental aspect of society is the starting point for applying the concepts from the toolbox and to start increasing one's agency in their construction of identity. The conceptual tools of social constructionism, ideology, and discourse help us to understand that such a social structure has material consequences. Recognizing that our society is constructed through social interactions allows us to see that our actions are not value neutral. When we understand that ideologies are cognitive organizing principles, then we can better comprehend how they inform our social interactions. Furthermore, by acknowledging that the mass-mediated texts that we consume, produce, and popularize are mundane manifestations of the normalized ideological systems of knowledge that we call "discourse," we can then be more intentional about engaging with popular media. From this perspective, we can productively utilize the tools of articulation, racial formation, whiteness, and otherness. Positioning media artifacts as sites of articulation helps us to identify and deconstruct the conceptual connections that the artifacts attempt to normalize. By examining these normalized connections, we are able to identify clearly how they perpetuate the racial formations that are often so common that they border on being invisible, yet are so influential that they shape the day-to-day structure of our lives. By revealing these racial formations, we can grapple with the conceptual whiteness at the core of the US racial project and at the same time engage with how that racial project positions people of color in general, and racialized Latinxs in particular, as constructed others. This brings us to the final two tools in the box, the narrative paradigm and suturing. Throughout the previous chapters, I have discussed the value of narratives, those that are mass mediated and those that are rooted in personal experience. I have also emphasized the relationship between the two, how narratives construct visions of our social world that provide us with language for constructing a sense of self while also navigating society. Ideally, by using the conceptual toolbox to arrive at the point of engaging with the social constructions of whiteness, otherness, and racialized *Latinidad*, we can parse apart the oppressive and emancipatory elements of mass-mediated narratives. By doing so, we can deconstruct the racist version of *Latinidad* that has been foisted upon us as Latinxs in the diaspora, the sort of falsehoods that facilitated my sense of internalized racism, and suture together a complex, dimensional, and dynamic identity.

The decision to identify in a way that is counter-hegemonic, that offers resistance to dominant racist constructions of *Latinidad*, also plays a role in the evolution of the US racial hierarchy. Whether people perceive us as Brown, Black, or White, when one's *Latinidad* is revealed, an entire set of identities and descriptors are ascribed based on the collective social conceptualization of what it means to be a part of that ethnic group. If I may borrow a line from the poem "Masks of Woman," by Mitsuye Yamada, to articulate this point, "Over my mask / is your mask / of me" (Allen, 2017). Every choice we make in terms of identity and expression exists in conversation with this system of racialization, and thus the choices we make are never neutral as they reinforce, modify, or subvert the aspects of identity forced on to us. By resisting the stereotypes associated with *Latinidad*, we disrupt the discourse that has shaped the perspectives of those outside of our communities.

At the same time, discourse about *Latinidad* comes as much from within our own communities as from outside of them. Each community has their own perspective on the validity of terms like Latino, Latina, Latinx, Latine, Latin@, or Hispanic. Some argue that using Latino as a collective term reinforces the patriarchy that has characterized much of the culture from Latin America. In response to that, some assert that we should use Latinx, although others insist this is a word invented by English speakers that is being forced onto us, even though there is no single, canonical origin for this term (at least not identified at the time of this writing). In this vein of thinking, some argue that we should use Latine because it makes more sense grammatically and phonetically in Spanish, but this has also been met with resistance by those who contend that gender-neutral language is inauthentic. And yet others maintain that we should not use any variation of these terms, or Hispanic, as they reflect an identity imposed by Spanish colonization. For my part, I use the term "Latinx" to refer to us as a collective and Latino to refer to myself, but I think the value of this term is not in and of itself but rather the exercise and process of experimentation. Maybe Latinx and Latine will last or maybe they won't, and certainly I think it is unreasonable to expect all of us to monolithically agree to a single term. I think that what is important is that we try to articulate ourselves, and that is a messy, nonlinear process. I cannot tell you what the correct identity is, only that choosing one is not value neutral and that no matter what you choose, one must still contend with the social construct of race.

The US racial order is only one macrolevel structure within which we must operate. Another is the system of *mestizaje* that has shaped much of Latin America and has taken root within the borders of the United States. *Mestizaje* does not map easily on to racial politics in the United States, as racial hybridity here is often seen as a novelty (even though it dates back to at least the colonial period), and those who are mixed are often identified with one side of their ancestry or the other. And while it is a legacy of Spanish colonialism, it is still something that Latinxs in the United States must navigate, even those of us who were born here. Within *mestizaje*, there is a dichotomy of the colonized and the colonizer (González, 2023), along with aspirational whiteness, anti-blackness, and Indigenous erasure (Olguín, 2013). And yet while this colonial ideology was instrumental to the development of normative, racially dominant, nationalist identities for Latin American countries in the way that whiteness was crafted for the United States, to embrace that nationalist identity in the United States further alienates a Latinx person as an other (Cisneros, 2011). But, as Anzaldua (2012) suggests, *mestizaje* is a *nepantla* space, a borderland between converging territories where we have to make choices about how we will express that internal borderland.

However, I want to be careful about leaning too hard into a *mestizaje* positionality. As Anzaldua (2012) asserts, this cognitive space can be useful for identifying one's Latinx ancestry as a series of intersecting forces that have led over time to one's current moment, and that by recognizing this, one can better understand their own identity and its inherent multiculturalism. But an uncritical application of this concept can lend itself to associating blood with race and culture in a way that is bio-essentialist and fetishizes ancestry, especially Indigeneity. So in order to protect against this type of problematic perspective, I think it is of value to interject Hall's concept of identity sutur-ing into *nepantla* and *mestizaje*. In his essay "Cultural Identity and Diaspora," Hall (1990) argues that there are, at least, two differing perspectives on how to think about cultural identity in the con-text of diasporic groups that have suffered colonization. The first is to think of cultural identity as a shared, collective, true version of the self that is rooted in a conceptualization of the past as being stable, recoverable, and unifying (Hall, 1990). This perspective is valuable for those who have lost their identity due to the horrors of colonization, but it is limiting. So, Hall (1990) argues in favor of the second perspective, which he views as more liberatory and open-ended, wherein cultural identity is positioned as a matter of navigating the convergence of the past and the present in a way that is perpetually renegotiated and transformed. This view of cultural identities considers them dynamic, constantly being made and unmade in response to the transformations of what we know, the dynamic discourses that shape society, and the futures we anticipate. From this perspective, Hall (1990) sees identities as "unstable points of identification, or suture, which are made, within the discourses of history and culture" (p. 226). Combining this idea of suturing together an identity from an unstable past, present, and future, with the interrogative critical consciousness of *mestizaje* can help us to navigate this moment as we consider where we come from and where we are going without attempt-ing to recreate a static sense of community that relies on a sta-ble, and at times fetishizing and reductive, conceptualization of history. With that in mind, let us consider the dynamic discourse of learned *Latinidad* as it relates to mass media.

Points to consider

In this book I have addressed how *Latinidad* is represented in the mass media of the United States through the news, fictional television and film, superhero narratives, and video games. I have discussed the tropes, stereotypes, and ideologies that inform these representations through a variety of theories and conceptual frameworks. Based on that material, there are a few key points that I want to emphasize as we consider how to move forward with navigating *Latinidad*.

The first point to consider is that through various forms of media, others, who are typically not a part of a Latinx community, have tried to instruct us on who we are. Media is a tool of learning about the world around us and about ourselves, and so we must consider what we have consumed and internalized, whether intentionally or not. For diaspora Latinxs who have grown up in the United States, the *Latinidad* that we have learned has not just been that which originates from our own ethnic groups. For example, I am Mexican American, and specifically, the *Mexicanos* that I come from and the *Mexicanidad* I claim are from the states of Durango and Chihuahua. They are *Norteños* who lived in rural places where agriculture was the primary way of making a living.. The racialized images and narratives designed to instruct me about myself in relation to my specific ethnic origins were often entirely negative if they were present at all. Instead, stereotypes like *cholos* in East Los Angeles, wearing flannel shirts and driving lowriders, or inner-city sex workers in any of the multitude of crime procedural shows on television, were more prevalent, and those images did not map onto my Latinx experience. These characters were a far cry from the men and women on my father's side of my family who worked outdoors with their hands or inside as domestic laborers. Furthermore, they were not authentic to the people they were attempting to depict. These were not humanizing, dimensional representations of reality; rather, they were cudgels that were used to tell us who we are and where we belonged in society.

Aside from the disparity in depictions of *Latinidad* on screen and my lived experience, there is also the matter of learning *Latinidad* from other Latinx communities. A Latinx person growing up in the United States might watch media starring actors from all over Latin America, like Sofia Vergara (Colombia), Oscar Isaac (Guatemala), Pedro Pascal (Chile), Morena Baccarin (Brazil), or Salma Hayek (Mexico). The characters that they play, whether they are meant to be representations of *Latinidad* or not, become examples of the kinds of Latinx people that we as a society value, and so we learn from them. Individually, these actors grapple with stereotypical and dimensional performances of *Latinidad*, whether overtly or implicitly, and thus can be positioned as role models or anti-models on a case-by-case basis. Taken collectively, they contribute to a milieu of pop culture *Latinidad* that is generic and thus both accessible and yet devoid of salient cultural distinctions that inform identity. In effect, we learn broad templates for how to perform *Latinidad* but without the particularities that speak to our diverse histories and lived experiences. As such, these tools for constructing a sense of *Latinidad* are limited in their use and are insufficient for helping us to create dimensional identities without supplementation.

The second point is that, while the majority of this book has been centered around understanding problematic conceptualizations of *Latindid* in mass media, progress has been made. Indeed, there is clear evidence for being optimistic about the future of *Latinidad* within mass media. Television/streaming series like the reboot of *One Day at a Time* (Kellet and Royce, 2017–2020) starring Rita Moreno, Justina Machado, Isabella Gomez, and Marcel Ruiz are proof that stories about Latinxs do not have to rely on hackneyed tropes and can still be compelling. *Coco* (Unkrich and Molina, 2017) and *Encanto* (Bush, Howard, and Smith, 2021) serve as strong examples of how Latinx cultural elements can serve as more than just narrative and visual window dressing in films; they can take center stage and be used to create immersive stories for Latinx and non-Latinx audiences alike. Comic book characters like DC's Jaime Reyes/Blue Beetle and Marvel's America Chavez illustrate that actual and metaphorical *Latinidad* is not just compatible with heroism, but these characters can also be valuable tools for engaging with real-world concerns and political issues. And while progress has been slow in the realm of video games, as González (2023) points out, stories like *Marvel's Spider-Man: Miles Morales* and *Life Is Strange 2*, while ideologically flawed in meaningful ways, represent shifts toward game developers being willing to place Latinxs as player characters. There is still room for growth and progress, and more than that there is a need for it, at the same time it is important to acknowledge the steps that have been taken and can hopefully be built upon.

The third point builds on the first and second points, and that is: we must be mindful that as we learn *Latinidad* from what has been represented to us, we do not fall into the trap of commodified, ornamental identity. Mass media projects are first and foremost capitalist endeavors, and as such the representation of identity can be a lucrative business in terms of selling merchandise and cultivating a fan following. And so, when we see mass-mediated representations of *Latinidad*, there are certain questions we should ask ourselves:

- If this depiction of *Latinidad* is supposed to be aimed at me, does it seem genuine?
- Is it a fabrication that serves ideological interests outside of that Latinx community?
- Am I familiar enough with this particular Latinx community to know the difference?
- Am I consuming this media because of the spectacle or because of personal resonance?
- Am I buying artifacts associated with that media as an effort to support and appreciate that culture or because I have fetishized it?
- Does my interest in that culture go beyond the moment of consumption, or does it carry into learning about that real-world group?

There are other questions to consider, such as who benefits monetarily from that consumption, whether there are creatives from that culture associated with the media, and so on. The questions that I have listed are a starting place for interrogating one's relationship with a piece of media that has been designed, at least in part, to be commodified and consumed.

The fourth and final key point to take away from the material covered in this book is that of expectations from dominant, mainstream mass media. Kristen J. Warner (2017) coined the term "plastic representation," which can be understood as "a combination of synthetic elements put together and shaped to look like meaningful imagery, but which can only approximate depth and substance because ultimately it is hollow and cannot survive close scrutiny" (para. 15). Warner (2017) argues that far too often diversity and representation are measured in terms of the number of actors and stories about people of color, and not often enough in terms of cultural specificity and depth. I am inclined to agree that mass media in a capitalist system is incentivized to operate in this way. Entertainment media studios use plastic representations to appeal to audience sensibilities and maintain their hegemonic influence on the industry, and news broadcasts engage in a variation of this by presenting stories that are about people of color which do not humanize them. Smaller, independent organizations have an interest in doing this as well in order to gain enough popularity and thus a foothold that will allow them to access the mainstream. This is not to say that genuine, humanizing representation cannot happen in mainstream mass media; clearly steps toward quality representations have been made. Plastic representation does not have to be the dominant mode of depicting racialized groups. As the media landscape continues to expand and fragment, allowing major corporations and small creators to experiment with entertainment media, there are growing opportunities for cultural producers to practice dimensional, humanizing representation of *Latinidad*. The profitability of niche audiences means that media companies no longer have to rely on the stereotypes discussed in this book that have been used to appeal to the broadest (read: White) audiences.

Moving forward

The subtitle of this volume, *Constructing Pocho Villa*, is more than just a mild joke at my expense; it is a sutured identity. For those who are not familiar, the word *pocho* is a derogatory term used to describe Americans of Mexican descent. On his website Pocho. com, the Mexican American cartoonist and satirist Lalo Alcaraz addresses the use of the term,

> Historically, a Pocho is an American of Mexican descent, considered by Mexicans to not be "Mexican" enough and by non-Mexicans of not being fully "American"—a citizen of two worlds but not really of either. At POCHO, we don't play that. We are re-imagining the word. We consider any Latino a POCHO if he belongs in BOTH worlds and wears BOTH identities proudly. You too, esteemed Latina ladies! (Pocho, n.d.)

This sentiment is reminiscent of Edward James Olmos's exasperated tirade in the film *Selena* (Nava, 1997) where he vents his frustration at how Mexican Americans must be perfect as Mexicans and Americans or be condemned as insufficient by both standards. Alcaraz's statement rejects the premise of being judged as lacking by the metrics of the two identities and instead reconceptualizes the term as a hybrid synthesis of the two. I used the surname *Villa* for this metaphorical character as a reference to the Mexican revolutionary Francisco "Pancho" Villa. I learned about this historical figure in middle school, and the idea of a Mexican bandit-turned-hero fighting to overthrow a tyrannical government left an impression on me. And while I have to acknowledge that the romanticized version of Villa that I was originally taught was significantly removed from the real person, I also must admit that in a world where the founding fathers of the United States are romanticized as nothing less than saviors, it was meaningful to know that Mexicans could be heroes in real life, too. So Pocho Villa represents a suturing together of Mexican-Americanness and institutional critique. I am both Mexican and American, yet I am not beholden to the standards of either. And just as Villa struggled against the Diaz regime of Mexico, I struggle against the regime of whiteness. But that is me. What about you?

If you are of Latin American origin or descent and are grappling with the idea of suturing together your own identity, there are a few things you may consider. The first is, do you need to be Latinx? What is the value of having a pan-ethnic identity term that encapsulates all of South, Central, and a third of North America? One could argue convincingly that having such a term runs the risk of homogenizing a territory that is almost incomprehensibly diverse, especially when the term is used by people outside of *Latinidad*. Terms like Latinx and Latine, or for that matter Latino/a and Hispanic, can easily serve as catch-all terms used by non-Latinxs who are only interested in learning about us as a conceptual group but not as people and communities. Furthermore, the idea of *Latinidad* is a colonial legacy. If the purpose of a term like Latinx is to disrupt the echoes of colonialism such as the linguistic patriarchy found in the Spanish language that enforces binary gender terms which favor masculinity, then should we be using any variation of Latino at all? Perhaps maintaining any pan-ethnic identity term that references Europe and thus the corresponding colonial history causes more problems than it solves. And yet, I think that such a term is not without merit. Using a word that is rooted in the term Latino meets us where we are as communities that are the product of the horrors of colonization. Whether we choose to accept or reject the ideological remnants of colonization that are entrenched in our respective cultures, the history of colonization in the Americas has left an indelible mark on those whose ancestry is rooted in Latin America. Both those of Indigenous descent who were detribalized through the project of *mestizaje* and the Indigenous Peoples who have survived and maintained a centuries-long resistance against the consequences of colonialism have been deeply shaped by colonization. Additionally, using a term like Latinx allows us to find each other in diaspora contexts, to express kinship, and build community around a common personal or ancestral origin in Latin America. This is exceedingly important for developing a sense of community strength and support in countries like the United States that insists on marginalizing Latinx people. Additionally, experimenting with the term "Latinx" prompts us to question *Latinidad*. Alan Pelaez Lopez, a nonbinary, Afro-Indigenous professor and artist, argues that the "X" in Latinx is symbolic of the scar left by the wounds inflicted by colonialism (Lopez, 2018). They assert that each point on the "X" stands for one of four wounds, anti-blackness, femicides, settlement, and inarticulation (the stripping away of language from Indigenous Peoples who were forced to speak Spanish and thus could not articulate their identities in the way that they originally had) (Lopez, 2018). As such, using the term "Latinx" helps us to engage with the legacies of colonialism and reflect on our own complicity in the maintenance of these oppressive systems.

With all of this in mind, I do not have a clear-cut answer for how to identify, nor am I prepared to prescribe one. As I mentioned earlier, I think the value of a concept like Latinx is less in the use of the term and more in the process of negotiating the ideological terrain that accompanies *Latinidad*, and so I return to Hall's (1990) idea of suturing. Approaching suturing through the concept of Latinx identity as understood by Lopez (2018) means reflecting on the colonial legacies that have become our birthright in the form of machismo, genocidal *mestizaje*, and other colonially based ideologies as we attempt to create a functional and affirming sense of self. Through this text I hope to have contributed to this suturing process by illustrating how mass media has played a role in the development of *Latinidad*, both on the macro- and microlevel, by providing us with language that more often than not reinforces a sense of alienation. Chicano journalist Ruben Salazar said that "A Chicano is a Mexican-American with a non-Anglo image of himself" (Salazar, 1970, para. 1). Consistent with the theme of this book, at the heart of this statement is the sentiment that we should be aware of how whiteness plays a role in how we see ourselves. Hopefully, through this book I have helped you to identify the media that alienates your sense of *Latinidad* while providing you with tools that you can use to create a more meaningful and empowering sutured identity.

Discussion questions

1. Given the colonial roots of *Latinidad*, can the concept be rearticulated into something counter-hegemonic? If so, how can we facilitate that process? If not, why?

2. Borrowing from the concept of "Player Juan" as how Latinxs are conceptualized as an audience by the video game industry, how do the other media industries addressed in this book conceptualize Latinx audiences?

3. With the understanding that the news media has become increasingly fragmented and our media ecosystem has made it easier for citizen journalism to grow, what ethical implications should a Latinx or non-Latinx citizen journalist consider when covering stories about Latinx communities?

4. Should we use cultural elements from real Latin American communities in the construction of superhero narratives and other forms of speculative fiction? Or is the risk that those elements will become fetishized too significant?

5. Why does children's media appear to allow for more dimensional representations of *Latinidad*? What lessons can be taken from that type of media and applied to entertainment for more mature audiences?

References

Aldama, F. L. (2009). *Your Brain on Latino Comics*. Austin: University of Texas Press.

Aldama, F. L. (2017). *Latinx Superheroes in Mainstream Comics*. Tuscon: University of Arizona Press.

Aldama, F. L., and Gonzalez, C. (2016). Latino Comic Books Past, Present, and Future—A primer. In: F. L. Aldama and C. Gonzalez, eds., *Graphic Borders: Latino Comic Books Past, Present, & Future*. Austin: University of Texas Press, pp. 1–21.

Aldama, F. L., and Gonzalez, C. (2019). *Reel Latinxs: Representation in U.S. Film and TV*. Tuscon:University of Arizona Press.

Allen, S. (2017). Free verse: Mitsuye Yamada, AM'53, Transformed Her Family's Internment Experience into Poetry. *UChicago Magazine, 109*(3). Available from: https://mag.uchicago.edu/university-news/free-verse [Accessed 10/01/2024]

Anders, A., Burgos, C., Everett, B., Gustavson, P., and Thompson, B. (1939). *Marvel Comics #1* [cartoon]. New York: Timely Comics.

Anzaldua, G. (2012). *Borderlands—La frontera: The New Mestiza*. 4th ed. San Francisco: Aunt Lute Books.

Appel, M. (2008). Fictional Narratives Cultivate Just-World Beliefs. *Journal of Communication, 58*, pp. 62–83.

Atkinson, J., and Calafell, B. (2009). "Darth Vader Made Me Do It!" Anakin Skywalker's Avoidance of Responsibility and the Gray Areas of Hegemonic Masculinity in the *Star Wars* Universe *Communication, Culture, & Critique, 2*, pp. 1–20.

Avilés-Santiago, M. G. (2019). Latina/os in media: Representation, production, and consumption. In: *Oxford Research*

Encyclopedias: Literature. Oxford: Oxford University Press. Available at: https://doi.org/10.1093/acrefore/9780190201098.013.389 [Accessed 11/18/2024]

Barbera, J. and Hanna W. (Directors). *Quick Draw McGraw.* (1959). [Television series]. United States: Hanna-Barbera Productions

Bebout, L. (2012). The Nativist Aztlán: Fantasies and Anxieties of Whiteness on the Border. *Latino Studies,* 10(3), pp. 290–313.

Bendis, B. M. (2013). *Ultimate Comics Spider-Man #22* [cartoon]. New York: Marvel.

Bendis, B. M. (2016a). *Spider-Man #6* [cartoon]. New York: Marvel.

Bendis, B. M. (2016b). *Spider-Man #10* [cartoon]. New York: Marvel.

Bogost, I. (2007). *Persuasive Games: The Expressive Power of Videogames.* Cambridge, MA: MIT Press.

Bond, S. (2023, April 25). How Tucker Carlson took fringe conspiracy theories to a mass audience. National Public Radio. Available at: https://www.npr.org/2023/04/25/1171800317/how-tucker-carlsons-extremist-narratives-shaped-fox-news-and-conservative-politi [Accessed 11/18/2024]

Bonilla-Silva, E. (2015). More Than Prejudice: Restatement, Reflections, and New Directions in Critical Race Theory. *Sociology of Race and Ethnicity,* 1(1), pp. 73–87.

Brayton, S. (2011). Razing Arizona: Migrant Labor and the "Mexican Avenger" of *Machete. International Journal of Media and Cultural Politics,* 7(3), pp. 275–292.

Brown, H. E., Jones, J. A., and Becker, A. (2018). The Racialization of Latino Immigrants in New Destinations: Criminality, Ascription, and Countermobilization. *RSF: The Russell Sage Foundation Journal of the Social Sciences,* 4(5), pp. 118–140. Available at: https://doi.org/10.7758/rsf.2018.4.5.06 [Accessed 11/18/2024]

Bucciferro, C. (2016). Introduction to: C. Bucciferro, ed., *The X-Men Films: A Cultural Analysis*. Lanham: Rowman & Littlefield, pp. ix–xxii.

Burgess, M. C. R., Dill, K. E., Stermer, P. Burgess, S. R., and Brown, B. P. (2011). Playing with Prejudice: The Prevalence and Consequences of Racial Stereotypes in Video Games. *Media Psychology*, 14(3), pp. 289–311.

Bush, J., Howard, B., and Smith, C. C. (Directors).. *Encanto*. (2021). [Film] United States: Walt Disney Animation Studios; Walt Disney Pictures.

Carpenter, M. J. (2021). Replaying Colonialism: Indigenous National Sovereignty and Its Limits in Strategic Videogames. *American Indian Quarterly*, 45(1), pp. 33–55.

Carrigan, W. D., and Webb, C. (2003). The Lynching of Persons of Mexican Origin or Descent in the United States, 1848 to 1928. *Journal of Social History*, 37(2), pp. 411–438.

Casillas, D. I., Ferrada, J. S., and Hinojos, S. V. (2018). The Accent on Modern Family: Listening to Representations of the Latina Vocal Body. *Aztlan: A Journal of Chicano Studies*, 43(1), pp. 61–87.

Cervantes, G. A., Alvord, D., and Menjivar, C. (2018). "Bad Hombres": The Effects of Criminalizing Latino Immigrants through Law and Media in the Rural Midwest. *Migration Letters*, 15(2), pp. 182–196.

Chambliss, J. C., Svitavsky, W., and Donaldson, T. (2013). Introduction to: J. C. Chambliss, W. Svitavsky, and T. Donaldson, eds., *Ages of Heroes, Eras of Men: Superheroes and the American Experience*. Newcastle: Cambridge Scholars, pp. 1–3.

Chess, S. (2017). *Ready Player Two: Women Gamers and Designed Identity*. Minneapolis: University of Minnesota Press.

Christiansen, J., Byrd, R., Couper-Smartt, J., Flamini, A., Hoskin, M., Lentz, B., McQuaid, S., Moreels, E. J., O'English, M., and Vandal, S.

(2005). *The Official Handbook of the Marvel Universe: Women of Marvel 2005*. New York: Marvel Comics.

Cisneros, J. D. (2008). Contaminated Communities: The Metaphor of "Immigrant as Pollutant" in Media Representations of Immigration. *Rhetoric and Public Affairs*, 11, pp. 569–602. Available at: https://doi.org/10.1353/rap.0.0068 [Accessed 11/18/2024]

Cisneros, J. D. (2011). (Re)bordering the Civic Imaginary: Rhetoric, Hybridity, and Citizenship in La Gran Marcha. *Quarterly Journal of Speech*, 97(1), pp. 26–49.

Cisneros, J. D. (2013). *The Border Crossed Us: Rhetorics of Borders, Citizenship, and Latina/o Identity*. Tuscaloosa: University of Alabama Press.

Clarke, J. (2015). Stuart Hall and the Theory and Practice of Articulation. *Discourse: Studies in the Cultural Politics of Education*, 36(2), pp. 275–286.

Coogler, R. (Director). *Black Panther: Wakanda Forever* (2022). [Film]. United States: Marvel Studio.

Cramer, L. M., Cruz, G. A., and Donofrio, A. R. (2023). Perpetual and Pleasurable Marginality: White Masculine Victimhood Appropriation and Black Masculine Sacrifice in Marvel's Netflix Series *The Punisher*. *Howard Journal of Communications*, 34(1), pp. 59–75. Available at: https://doi.org//10.1080/10646175.2022.2090032 [Accessed 11/18/2024]

Cravey, A. J. (1997). Latino Labor and Poultry Production in rural North Carolina. *Southeastern Geographer*, 37(2), pp. 295–300. Available at: https://doi.org/10.1353/sgo.1997.0001 [Accessed 11/18/2024]

Cruz, G. A. (2021). My bloodright: A critical analysis of *Black Panther's* Erik Killmonger, colonialism, and hybrid identity. In: R. T. White and K. A. Ritzenhoff, eds., *Afrofuturism in Black Panther: Gender, Identity and the Re-Making of Blackness*. Lanham: Lexington Books, pp. 315–332.

Cuadros, P. (2006). *A Home on the Field: How One Championship Team Inspires Hope for the Revival of Small Town America.* New York: Harper Collins.

D'Amore, L. M. (2008). Invisible Girl's Quest for Visibility: Early Second Wave Feminism and the Comic Book Superheroine. *Americana,* 7(2), pp. 3–11.

Deckard, N. D., Browne, I., Rodriguez, C., Martinez-Cola, M., and Leal, S. G. (2020). Controlling Images of Immigrants in the Mainstream and Black Press: The Discursive Power of the "Illegal Latino." *Latino Studies,* 18, pp. 581–602. Available at: https://doi.org/10.1057/s41276-020-00274-4 [Accessed 11/18/2024]

Dickerman, C., Christensen, J., and Kerl-McClain, S. B. (2008). Big Breasts and Bad Guys: Depictions of Gender and Race in Video Games. *Journal of Creativity in Mental Health,* 3(1), pp. 20–29.

Dunaway, J., Goidel, R. K., Kirzinger, A., and Wilkinson, B. C. (2011). Rebuilding or Intruding? Media Coverage and Public Opinion on Latino Immigration in Post-Katrina Louisiana. *Social Science Quarterly,* 92(4), pp. 917–937. Available at: https://doi: 10.1111/j.1540-6237.2011.00797.x [Accessed 11/18/2024]

Entertainment Software Association. (2024) *Essential facts about the U.S. video game industry.* Available at: https://www.theesa.com/resources/essential-facts-about-the-us-video-game-industry/2024-data/ [Accessed 11/18/2024]

Erba, J. (2018). Media Representations of Latina/os and Latino Students' Stereotype Threat Behavior. *Howard Journal of Communications,* 29(1), pp. 83–102. Available at: https://doi.org/10.1080/10646175.2017.1327377 [Accessed 11/18/2024]

Espinoza, M. (2016). The alien is here to stay: Otherness, anti-assimilation, and empowerment in Latino/a superhero comics. In: F. L. Aldama and C. Gonzalez, eds., *Graphic Borders: Latino Comic Books Past, Present, & Future.* Austin: University of Texas Press, pp. 181–202.

Everett, A., and Watkins, S. G. (2008). The power of play: The portrayal and performance of race in video games. In: K. Salen, ed., *The Ecology of Games: Connecting Youth, Games, and Learning.* Cambridge, MA: MIT Press, pp. 141–166.

Fellow, S., Bollen, R., and Sadler, M. (Creators). *Handy Manny.* (2006). [Television series]. United States: Disney Enterprises

Fernandez, D. (2014, May). Immigrant deportations today and the continuing legacy of "Operation Wetback." Origins: Current Events in Historical Perspective. Available at: https://origins.osu.edu/milestones/may-2014-immigrant-deportations-today-and-continuing-legacy-operation-wetback?language_content_entity=en [Accessed 11/18/2024]

Figueroa-Caballero, A., and Mastro, D. (2019). Examining the Effects of News Coverage Linking Undocumented Immigrants with Criminality: Policy and Punitive Implications. *Communication Monographs,* 86(1), pp. 46–67. Available at: https://doi.org/10.1080/03637751.2018.1505049 [Accessed 11/18/2024]

Figueroa-Caballero, A., Mastro, D., and Stamps, D. (2019). An Examination of the Effects of Mediated Intragroup and Intergroup Interactions among Latino/a Characters. *Communication Quarterly,* 67(3), pp. 271–290. Available at: https://doi.org/10.1080/01463373.2019.1573745 [Accessed 11/18/2024]

Fisher, W. R. (1984). Narration as a Human Communication Paradigm: The Case of Public Moral Argument. *Communication Monographs,* 51, pp. 1–22.

Fisher, W. R. (1985). The Narrative Paradigm: An Elaboration. *Communication Monographs,* 52, pp. 347–367.

Flores, L. A. (2016). Between Abundance and Marginalization: The Imperative of Racial Rhetorical Criticism. *Review of Communication,* 16(1), pp. 4–24. Available at: https://doi.org/10.1080/15358593.2016.1183871 [Accessed]11/18/2024

Forte, D., Dorta, C., and Richman, B. A. (Creators). *Maya & Miguel*. (2004). [Television series]. United States: Scholastic

Frank, K. M. (2016) Everybody wants to rule the multiverse: Latino Spider-Men in Marvel's media empire. In: F. L. Aldama and C. Gonzalez, eds., *Graphic Borders: Latino Comic Books Past, Present, & Future*. Austin: University of Texas Press, pp. 241–251.

Freleng, F. (Director). *Speedy Gonzales*. (1955). [Film]. United States: Warner Bros. Cartoon Studios

Giacchino, M. (Director). *Werewolf by Night* (2022). [Film]. United States: Marvel Studios.

Gledhill, H. E. (2016). Superhuman authority: Fascism and bioethics in the X-Men films. In: C. Bucciferro, ed., *The X-Men Films: A Cultural Analysis*. Lanham: Rowman & Littlefield, pp. 33–47.

Gonzalez, A., Chávez, J., and Englebrecht, C.M. (2014). *Latinidad and Vernacular Discourse: Arts Activism in Toledo's Old South End. Journal of Poverty*, 18(1), pp. 50–64. Available at: https://doi.org/10.1080/10875549.2013.866805 [Accessed 11/18/2024]

González, C. G. K. (2023). *Ready Player Juan: Latinx Masculinities and Stereotypes in Video Games*. Tucson: University of Arizona Press.

Gonzalez-Sobrino, B. (2020). Searching for the "Sleeping Giant": Racialized News Coverage of Latinos pre-2020 Elections. *Sociological Forum*, 35(S1), pp. 1019–1039. Available at: https://doi: 10.1111/socf.12605 [Accessed 11/18/2024]

Gray, G. L., and Leonard, D. J. (2018). Not a post-racism and post-misogyny promised land: Video games as instruments of (in)justice. In: G. L. Gray and D. J. Leonard, eds., *Woke Gaming: Digital Challenges to Oppression and Social Injustice*. Seattle: University of Washington Press, pp. 3–23.

Grimwood, T. (2018). Procedural Monsters: Rhetoric, Commonplace and "Heroic Madness" in Video Games. *Journal of Cultural Research*, 22(3), pp. 310–324.

Guess, T. J. (2006). The Social Construction of Whiteness: Racism by Intent, Racism by Consequence. *Critical Sociology*, 32(4), pp. 649–673.

Guxens, A. (2012, October 7). George R.R. Martin: "trying to please everyone is a horrible mistake." Adria's News. Available at: http://www.adriasnews.com/2012/10/george-r-r-martin-interview.html [Accessed 11/18/2024]

Guynes, S., and Lund, M. (2020). Not to interpret but to abolish: Whiteness studies and American superhero comics. In: S. Guynes and M. Lund, eds., *Unstable Masks: Whiteness and American Superhero Comics*. Columbus: Ohio State University Press, pp. 1–16.

Hall, S. (1990). Cultural identity and diaspora. In: J. Rutherford, ed., *Identity: Community, Culture, Difference*. London: Lawrence & Wishart, pp. 222–235.

Hall, S. (2019). On postmodernism and articulation: An interview with Stuart Hall by Larry Grossberg and others [1986]. In: D. Morley, ed., *Essential Essays Vol. 1: Foundations of Cultural Studies*. Durham: Duke University Press, pp. 222–246.

Heuman, A. N., and Gonzalez, A. (2018) Trump's Essentialist Border Rhetoric: Racial Identities and Dangerous Liminalities. *Journal of Intercultural Communication Research*, 47(4), pp. 326–342.

Hirsch, P. (2014). "This is our enemy": The Writer's War Board and Representations of Race in Comic Books, 1942–1945. *Pacific Historical Review*, 83(3), 448–486.

Hitch, B. (2017). *Justice League #26* [cartoon]. Burbank, CA: DC Comics.

Holthouse, D. (2005, June 27). Minutemen, other anti-immigrant militia groups stake out Arizona border. Southern Poverty Law Center. Available at: https://www.splcenter.org/fighting-hate/intelligence-report/2005/minutemen-other-anti-immigrant-militia-groups-stake-out-arizona-border [Accessed 11/18/2024]

Huber, L. P., and Solorzano, D. G. (2015). Visualizing Everyday Racism: Critical Race Theory, Visual Microaggressions, and the Historical Image of Mexican Banditry. *Qualitative Inquiry*, 21(3), pp. 223–238. Available at: https://doi.org/10.1177/107780041 4562899 [Accessed 11/18/2024]

Hudson, R. (2019, December 2). Imagining the Futures of Latinx Speculative Fictions. *ASAP/Review*. Available at: https://asapjour nal.com/feature/imagining-the-futures-of-latinx-speculative-fictions-renee-hudson/ [Accessed May 20, 2024]

Human Rights Watch. (2023). *Statement of Humans Rights Watch: The human cost of harsh US immigration deterrence policies before the US House Homeland Security Committee*. Human Rights Watch. Available at: https://www.hrw.org/news/2023/07/26/ statement-human-rights-watch-human-cost-harsh-us-immigrat ion-deterrence-policies [Accessed 11/18/2024]

Jones, G. (1989). *El Diablo #1* [cartoon]. New York: DC Comics.

Kellet, G. C., and Royce, M. (Creators). (2017–2020). *One Day at a Time* [TV series]. Act III Productions; GloNation Studios; Snowpants Productions.

Lopez, A. P. (2018, September). The x in Latinx is a wound, not a trend. ColorBloq. Available at: https://colorbloq-qtpoc-4011.squa respace.com/the-x-in-latinx-is-a-wound-not-a-trend [Accessed 11/18/2024]

Kesel, K. (1997a). *Superboy and the Ravers #13* [cartoon]. New York: DC Comics.

Kesel, K. (1997b). *Superboy and the Ravers #14* [cartoon]. New York: DC Comics.

Killen, K, and Kane, S. (Writers), and Bathurst, O. (Director). (2022, March 24). *Contact* (Season 1 Episode 1) [TV series episode]. In: O. Bathurst (Executive Producer), *Halo*. 343 Industries; Amblin Television; Chapter Eleven.

Klein, B. (2024, February 5). How Blue Beetle fits into James Gunn's DCU plans cautiously addressed by Xolo Maridueña. Screen Rant. Available at: https://screenrant.com/blue-beetle-james-gunn-dcu-plans-xolo-mariduena-response/ [Accessed 11/18/2024]

Kinefuchi, E., and Cruz, G. (2015). The Mexicans in the News: Representation of Mexican Immigrants in the Internet News Media. *Howard Journal of Communications,* 26, pp. 333–351.

Lacy, M. G., and Haspel, K. C. (2011). Apocalypse: The media's framing of Black looters, shooters, and brutes in Hurricane Katrina's aftermath. In: M. G. Lacy and K. A. Ono, eds., *Critical Rhetorics of Race*. New York: New York University Press, pp. 21–46.

Leonard, D. (2003). "Live in Your World, Play in Ours": Race, Video Games, and Consuming the Other. *Studies in Media & Information Literacy Education,* 3(4), pp. 1–9.

Library of Congress. (n.d.). 1994: California's Proposition 187. A Latinx Resource Guide: Civil Rights Cases and Events in the United States. Available at: https://guides.loc.gov/latinx-civil-rights/california-proposition-187#s-lib-ctab-25769023-2 [Accessed 11/18/2024]

Lin, B. (2023, February 22). *Diversity in Gaming Report: An Analysis of Diversity in Video Game Characters*. Diamond Lobby. Available at: https://diamondlobby.com/geeky-stuff/diversity-in-gaming/ [Accessed 11/18/2024]

Lobdell, S. (201). *Teen Titans Vol. 4 #30* [cartoon]. New York: DC Comics.

Loomba, A. (2005). *Colonialism/Postcolonialism.* 2nd ed. New York: Routledge.

Lopez, L. K. (2020). Racism and mainstream media. In: L. K. Lopez, ed., *Race and Media: Critical Approaches*. New York: New York University Press, pp. 13–26.

Luo, Y., Burley, H., Moe, A., and Sui, M. (2019). A Meta-analysis of News Media's Public Agenda-Setting Effects, 1972–2015.

Journalism & Mass Communication Quarterly, 96(1), 150–172. Available at: https://doi.org/10.1177/1077699018804500 [Accessed 11/18/2024]

Mastro, D., Behm-Morawitz, E., and Ortiz, M. (2007). The Cultivation of Social Perceptions of Latinos: A Mental Models Approach. *Media Psychology,* 9, pp. 347–365.

McGrath, K. (2007). Gender, Race, and Latina Identity: An Examination of Marvel Comics' Amazing Fantasy and Araña. *Atlantic Journal of Communication,* 15(4), pp. 268–283.

Millán, I. (2016). Anya Sofia (Araña) Corazón: The inner webbings and Mexi-Ricanization of Spider-Girl. In: F. L. Aldama and C. Gonzalez, eds., *Graphic Borders: Latino Comic Books Past, Present, & Future.* Austin: University of Texas Press, pp. 203–223.

Montes, B. (2016). The paradox of Miles Morales: Social gatekeeping and the browning of America's Spider-Man. In F. L. Aldama and C. Gonzalez, eds., Graphic Borders: Latino Comic Books Past, Present, & Future. Austin: University of Texas Press, pp. 269–279

Murray, S. (2018). *On Video Games: The Visual Politics of Race, Gender and Space.* London: I. B. Tauris.

Nakayama, T. K., and Krizek, R. L. (1995). Whiteness: A Strategic Rhetoric. *Quarterly Journal of Speech,* 81, pp. 291–309.

Nama, A. (2011). *Super Black: American Pop Culture and Black Superheroes.* Austin: University of Texas Press.

Nama, A., and Haddad, M. (2016). Mapping the *Blatino* badlands and borderlands of American pop culture. In: F. L. Aldama and C. Gonzalez, eds., *Graphic Borders: Latino Comic Books Past, Present, & Future.* Austin: University of Texas Press, pp. 252–268.

Nava, G. (Director). *Selena* (1997). [Film]. United States: Q Productions; Esparza/Katz Productions.

Navarro, S. V. (2017). The Silent Other in Contemporary Border Cinema: The Latino Figure in No Country for Old Men and

The Three Burials of Melquiades Estrada. *Latino Studies,* 15, pp. 309–322.

Novak, N. L., Lira, N., O'Connor, K. E., Harlow, S. D., Kardia, S. L. R., and Stern, A. M. (2018). Disproportionate Sterilizations of Latinos under California's Eugenic Sterilization Program, 1920–1945. *American Journal of Public Health,* 108(5), pp. 611–613.

Oh, D. C., and Kutufam, D. V. (2014). The Orientalized "other" and Corrosive Femininity: Threats to White Masculinity in 300. *Journal of Communication Inquiry,* 38(2), pp. 149–165.

Olguín, B. V. (2013). *Caballeros* and Indians: Mexican American Whiteness, Hegemonic Mestizaje, and Ambivalent Indigeneity In Proto-Chicana/o Autobiographical Discourse, 1858–2008. *MELUS,* 38(1), pp. 30–49.

Omi, M., and Winant, H. (2015). *Racial Formations in the United States.* New York: Routledge

O'Neill, S. (2019, May 31). Who Threw the First Brick at Stonewall? Let's Argue about It. *New York Times.* Available at: https://www.nytimes.com/2019/05/31/us/first-brick-at-stonewall-lgbtq.html [Accessed May 16, 2024]

Oyola, O. (2020). Marked for failure: Whiteness, innocence, and power in defining Captain America. In: S. Guynes and M. Lund, eds., *Unstable Masks: Whiteness and American Superhero Comics.* Columbus: Ohio State University Press, pp. 19–37.

Planas, M. C. (2021). Superheroine Latinidad: The diasporic identities of America Chavez & La Borinqueña. *Journal of Popular Culture,* 54(5), pp. 1012–1030.

Penix-Tadsen, P. (2016). *Cultural Code: Video Games and Latin America.* Cambridge, MA: MIT Press.

Penix-Tadsen, P. (2013). Latin American Ludology: Why We Should Take Video Games Seriously (and When We Shouldn't). *Latin American Research Review,* 48(1), pp. 174–190.

Pocho. (n.d.). *¿Y que? What is this thing called POCHO?* Available at: https://www.pocho.com/about/ [Accessed 11/18/2024]

Priest, C. (2019). *Justice League #38* [cartoon]. Burbank, CA: DC Comics.

Ramirez-Berg, C. (2002). *Latino Images in Film: Stereotypes, Subversion, & Resistance.* Austin: University of Texas Press.

Rodriguez, R. T. (2016). Revealing secret identities: Gay Latino superheroes and the necessity of disclosure. In: F. L. Aldama and C. Gonzalez, eds., *Graphic Borders: Latino Comic Books Past, Present, & Future.* Austin: University of Texas Press, pp. 224–237.

Rucka, G. (2003). *Gotham Central #10* [cartoon]. New York: DC Comics.

Rudolph, J. D. (2017). "Whose Manhattan?": Mapping Color-Blind Justice for Latinos on Law & Order. *Journal of Popular Culture,* 50(5), pp. 983–1002.

Russworm, T. M. (2017). Dystopian blackness and the limits of racial empathy in *The Walking Dead* and *The Last of Us*. In: J. Malkowski and T. M. Russworm, eds., *Gaming Representation: Race, Gender, and Sexuality in Video Games.* Bloomington: Indiana University Press, pp. 109–128.

Salazar, R. (1970, Feb. 6.). The Ruben Salazar Collection of Opinion Articles: "Border Correspondent.". *Column: Who is Chicano? And What is it The Chicanos Want?.* The California-Mexico Studies Center. Available at: https://www.california-mexicocenter.org/the-ruben-salazar-collection-of-opinion-articles-border-corres pondent/#:~:text=A%20Chicano%20is%20a%20Mexican,to%20 the%20%E2%80%9CNew%20World.%E2%80%9D [Accessed 11/18/2024]

Santa Ana, O. (2013) *Juan in a Hundred.* Austin: University of Texas Press.

Santos, J. J. (2021). Talented tensions and revisions: The narrative double consciousness of Miles Morales. In: S. A. Dagbovie-Mullins and E. L. Berlatsky, eds., *Mixed-Race Superheroes*. New Brunswick, NJ: Rutgers University Press, pp. 179–198.

Santos, J. D., Power, K., Thompson, J. K. (Directors). *Spider-Man: Across the Spider-Verse*. (2023). [Film]. United States: Columbia Pictures.

Scheufele, D. A., and Tewksbury, D. (2007). Framing, Agenda Setting, and Priming: The Evolution of Three Media Effects Models. *Journal of Communication*, 57, pp. 9–20. Available at: https://doi:10.1111/j.1460-2466.2006.00326.x [Accessed 11/18/2024]

Scott, S. (2015). The Hawkeye Initiative: Pinning Down Transformative Feminisms in Comic-Book Culture through Superhero Crossplay Fan Art. *Cinema Journal*, 55(1), pp. 150–160.

Sellnow, D. D. (2017). *The Rhetorical Power of Popular Culture: Considering Mediated Texts*. 3rd ed. Thousand Oaks: Sage.

Skidmore, M. J. and Skidmore, J. (1983). More Than Mere Fantasy: Political Themes in Contemporary Comic Books. *Journal of Popular Culture*, 18, pp. 83–92.

Slack, J. D. (1996). The theory and method of articulation in cultural studies. In: D. Morley and K. H. Chen, eds., *Stuart Hall: Critical Dialogues in Cultural Studies*. New York: Routledge, pp. 113–127.

Soto, A. M. (Director). *Blue Beetle*. (2023). [Film]. United States: Warner Bros.

Squires, E., Stone, J,. Simon, L., and May, T. (Directors). (1991). Episode #2888 [Television series episode]. In D. Singer (Producer), *Sesame Street*. United States: Sesame Workshop

Stamps, D. (2019). Is It Really Representation? A Qualitative Analysis of Asian and Latino Characterizations in Broadcast Television. *American Communication Journal*, 21(1), pp. 1–12.

Swift, T. (2015, February 10). The case for a non-white Spider-Man. *BBC*. Available at: https://www.bbc.com/news/blogs-trending-31362800 [Accessed May 16, 2024]

Tukachinsky, R., Mastro, D., and Yarchi, M. (2017). The Effect of Prime Time Television Ethnic/Racial Stereotypes on Latino and Black Americans: A Longitudinal National Level Study. *Journal of Broadcasting & Electronic Media,* 61(3), pp. 538–556. Available at: https://doi.org/10.1080/08838151.2017.1344669 [Accessed 11/18/2024]

Unkrich, L., and Molina, A. (Directors). *Coco.* (2017). [Film]. United States: Walt Disney Pictures; Pixar Animation Studios; Dia de Muertos.

US Census Bureau. (2021, August 4). *Measuring Racial and Ethnic Diversity for the 2020 Census.* Available at: https://www.census.gov/newsroom/blogs/random-samplings/2021/08/measuring-racial-ethnic-diversity-2020-census.html#:~:text=The%20Wh ite%20alone%2C%20non%2DHispanic,third%2Dlargest%20 at%2012.2%25 [Accessed 11/18/2024]

US Department of Commerce. (1990). *1990 Census of Population: General Population Characteristics: North Carolina. Available at:* https://www2.census.gov/library/publications/decennial/1990/cp-1/cp-1-35.pdf [Accessed 11/18/2024]

US Department of State. (n.d.). *The Immigration Act of 1924 (The Johnson-Reed Act).* Office of the Historian. Available at: https://history.state.gov/milestones/1921-1936/immigration-act [Accessed 11/18/2024]

US Immigration and Customs Enforcement. (n.d.). *Delegation of Immigration Authority Section 287(g) Immigration and Nationality Act.* Available at: https://www.ice.gov/identify-and-arrest/287g [Accessed 11/18/2024]

Valdes, V. W. and Gifford, C. (Creators). *Go, Diego! Go!.* (2005). [Television series]. United States: Nick Jr. Productions

Valdez, C. (2024, March 26). Indigenous representation in video games. Cultural Survival. Available at: https://www.culturalsurvival.org/news/indigenous-representation-video-games#:~:text= Portrayals%20of%20Indigenous%20Peoples%20relied,of%20Nat ive%20Americans%20in%20media [Accessed 11/18/2024]

Warner, K. J. (2017, December 4). Plastic Representation. *Film Quarterly*, 71(2). Available at: https://filmquarterly.org/2017/12/04/in-the-time-of-plastic-representation/#:~:text=An%20operational%20definition%20of%20plastic,and%20cannot%20survive%20close%20scrutiny [Accessed 11/18/2024]

Weiner, E., Gifford, C., and Valdes, V. W. (Creators). *Dora the Explorer*. (2000). [Television series]. United States: Nick Jr. Productions

Wijman, T. (2024, February 8). Newzoo's games market revenue estimates and forecasts by region and segment for 2023. Newzoo. Available at: https://newzoo.com/resources/blog/games-market-estimates-and-forecasts-2023 [Accessed 11/18/2024]

Williams, D., Martins, N., Consalvo, M., and Ivory, J. D. (2009). The Virtual Census: Representations of Gender, Race, and Age in Video Games. *New Media & Society*, 11(5), pp. 815–834.

Index

www.ingramcontent.com/pod-product-compliance
Lightning Source LLC
Chambersburg PA
CBHW070334270326
41926CB00017B/3873